EGYPT
Land of the Valley

EGYPT
Land of the Valley

———◆·•·◆———

ROBIN FEDDEN

JOHN MURRAY

103979

Printed in Great Britain by
The Camelot Press Ltd, Southampton
0 7195 3342 2

To Susan

Contents

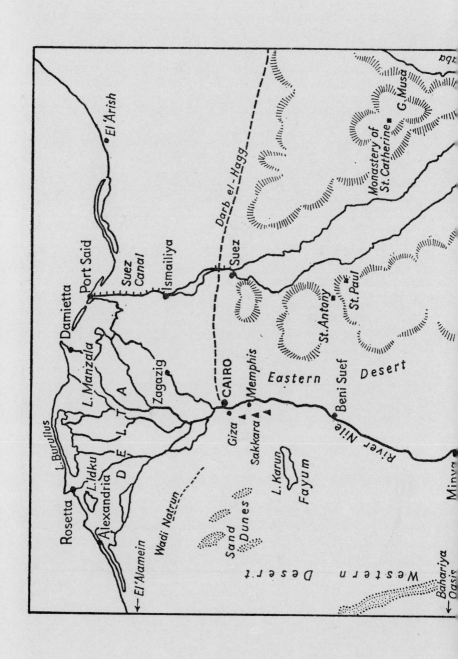

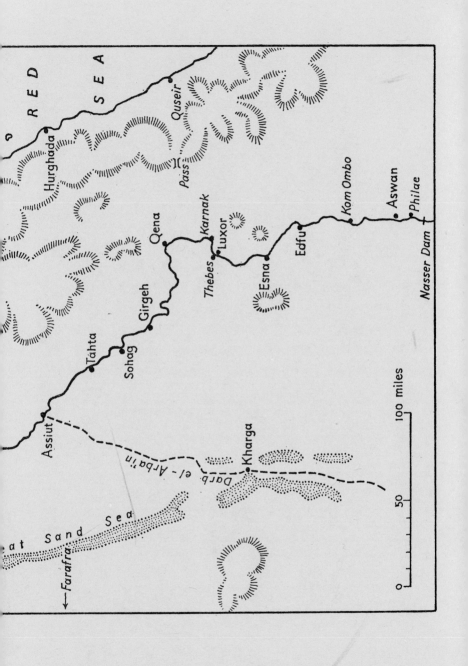

Illustrations

———◆•••◆———

SOURCES OF PLATES

Acknowledgements are due to the following: Middle East Archive, jacket front and 2, 18, 19, 20; A. Costa, jacket back and 3, 9, 10, 11, 14, 15, 16, 17, 21, 24, 25, 27, 28, 32; Aerofilms, 13; Alban, 5, 6, 22 (Egypt State Tourist), 23; Robin Fedden, 7, 26; Geoffrey Fielden, 4, 29, 30; Lee Miller, 8; Hella Sachs, 1, 12, 31.

MAPS

The general map of Egypt between pages 8 and 9 and the map of Old Cairo on page 98 were drawn by K. C. Jordan.

ONE

The Country and the Traveller

The oracle of Jupiter-Ammon from its Saharan oasis pronounced centuries ago that 'Egypt was the entire tract of country which the Nile overspreads and irrigates, and the Egyptians were the people who lived below Elephantine and drank the waters of that river.' Though not altogether accurate, the definition is pleasing, and the oracle shrewdly linked Egypt and the Egyptian indissolubly to the Nile. It was Nile silt that stole the Delta from the sea, thus creating two-thirds of the country's arable land. Today the mariner taking soundings when still a good day's sail from the coast brings up on his line, not the legitimate gravels of the deep, but black Nile mud. This is a sediment perfectly symbolic of the land for which his sails are set. The Nile conditions Egypt and there is no escaping its authority. Though a comparative parvenu among rivers, forcing its way among hills and landscapes infinitely more ancient, it yet exerts a greater influence on a greater number of people than Amazons and Mississippis of older geographical standing. This single stream is in Egypt the first source of existence for nearly 40 million people. For millennia life and death, feast and famine, were foretold in the measure of its flood. Crime rose and fell inversely to the water, and virtues blossomed because of Abyssinian rains. The Beduin creeping down from the desert to sustain existence on the cultivation's edge and the Egyptian cotton market are alike subject to the river.

In ancient times the Nile took its place with the gods, and in the river's annual rising were seen the tears of the blessed Isis weeping for Osiris. It was also regarded as the origin of life and from its breathless mud were generated insect, bird, beast and man. Today water—the water of the Nile—is the last ritual draught offered to the dying Egyptian Muslim. The Nile is with these people from birth to death.

Yet the Nile alone is not Egypt. The country, its pronounced flavour and its distinctive works, is an eternal amalgam of two things: the river and the toilers on its banks. Only by the co-operation of the fellah, who is an element as essential as the river and who seems almost as permanent, are 5,000 years of history explained. The conjunction of these two, and their troubled contacts with the outside world, have created Egypt from Aswan to the sea. They conditioned the landscape, and set the pyramids beyond the floodland; they stamp everything with its particular Egyptian quality, indefinable but patent. They differentiate the mosques of Cairo from those of Isfahan, they make the warp in Egypt go up not down the woof, and turn the matter of Plato into the speculation of Plotinus.

Into the midst of this people and landscape aliens have come for wealth or power, to found dynasties or run groceries, but in the end they pay a price for their invasion; they lose their identity, they are submerged by those whom they have conquered or exploited. The many Greek soldiers whom a benevolent Ptolemy settled in the Fayum have left no trace, no trick of custom or Aegean feature, in that district. The Libyans who gave them a desert dynasty, the Ptolemies who gave them style, and the Arabs who brought a new faith, are, with all the rest, long since racially obliterated. Like pebbles thrown into a pond, they only wrinkled the surface.

Veneers of thought from abroad, now imported on aircraft and steamers but once entering the Nile by trireme and dhow, lose their lustre. Distorted, or improved, they become unrecognizable and the native way of thought prevails. Successively the dominant aliens pass; their memory survives in stone monuments, for which the Egyptian has a characteristic disregard. Like the gigantic bird migrations that sweep up the Nile valley, passing out of sight into the obscure tropical south, the storming foreigners leave in their wake a country essentially unchanged. Egypt is averse, as Herodotus once found it, to being anything but Egypt.

The upper stratum of society may alter—pharaoh, caliph, pasha, or prime minister, may affect a foreign mode—but the character of the country, its being, remains unaffected. Hence the impressive sense of permanence and duration. A continuity links the ruined temple to the descendants of the fellahin who built it. The legacies of Ancient and Medieval Egypt are witness to a timeless existence, now as long ago product of the river and the human figures on the banks.

Though Ptolemy and caliph, Turk and Briton, disappear, the traveller in Egypt never fails. The Greeks broke the ground, a host of tourists whetting an Aegean curiosity. Later the Romans flocked to see the sights and carve their names on public monuments. In the Middle Ages, Von Suchem was moved to wonder at the 'little green parroquet birds' on the Nile, and Antoninus Martyr piously visited the tombs of Alexandrian saints. The first visitor from the British Isles whose name is known to us was probably the monk Pelagius, who arrived in about A.D. 400 propounding an attractive doctrine that may be summarized in the phrase, 'If I ought, I can.' So bold a reliance on free will left little scope for divine grace, and Pelagius found himself a heretic. In succeeding centuries, with the great increase in pilgrim traffic to Jerusalem, other Britons passed through, and in the 14th century two at least paid a visit to that ancient Christian shrine, the church of Abu Sargah in Cairo. British Crusaders landed with less innocent intent. At the siege of Damietta in 1218 the Earl of Chester was 'marvellously commended of all men', and at the wanton sack of Alexandria in 1365 a Scot was the first man to scale the walls.

But it was only with the creation of the Levant Company in 1581, a reflection of the bold spirit of maritime and commercial enterprise that sent the Elizabethans round the globe, and the subsequent establishment of a consulate in Cairo, that Egypt began to be reasonably accessible to the traveller from Britain. The poet George Sandys climbed the Great Pyramid in the year that Shakespeare retired to Stratford, and John Greaves, later Professor of Astronomy at Oxford, measured the pyramids in the 1630s. Sandys's account of his travels went into nine editions, and before the end of the 17th century some dozen Englishmen had published descriptions of Cairo and Alexandria. It was not long before Egypt was an ambitious extension to the Grand Tour. The Earl of Sandwich dropped anchor at Alexandria in his private yacht in 1738, and about the same time Richard Pococke, the ecclesiastic whose 'superior learning and dignity' impressed Gibbon, reached the temple of Philae beyond the first cataract. By the end of the 18th century some twenty English travellers had carved their names on the Great Pyramid. The winter season was almost in sight.

The traveller is free; he is a member of no specific society or generation. No routine constricts him, he has escaped from relentlessly familiar faces and places. He enjoys the illusion that he is unpegged in time. His personality grows elastic, can stretch from century to century.

Some countries confer this sense of freedom better than others. Egypt, with its enormous time-span and weird contrasts, is peculiarly fitted to do so. For 2,000 years and more it has been the traveller's goal.

In the latter half of the 19th century the traveller in Egypt combined romance with comfort perhaps better than he ever did before or will do again. Even the non-entity might shoot crocodiles and return laden with mummies. Persons of consequence, with the proper letters of introduction, dined cross-legged in Turkish splendour, picnicked off gold plate beside the Sphinx, and enjoyed the sight of barefoot syces in red velvet running before their carriages. Accommodating hosts would arrange for the enthusiastic amateur of Egyptology to discover a tomb which, with Oriental courtesy, had been prepared overnight. Few visitors, however, can have progressed as luxuriously up the Nile as the Prince and Princess of Wales in 1869. On February 6th, as the guests of the Khedive Ismail, they left Cairo with their suite—it included Sir Samuel Baker who had travelled in less comfortable circumstances to discover the source of the Nile—in six blue and gold steamers whose interior decoration illustrated the theme of Antony and Cleopatra. Each steamer towed 'a barge filled with luxuries and necessities including four riding horses, and a milk-white donkey for the Princess; 3,000 bottles of champagne and 4,000 of claret; four French chefs and a laundry'.* When the royal couple returned in mid-March it was 'with 32 mummy cases, an immense sarcophagus, and a 10-year-old chocolate-coloured orphan boy, Ali Achmet'. The last was dispatched to Sandringham, where he served coffee in native dress.

Though nowadays time and money rarely launch private

* See Philip Magnus, *King Edward the Seventh*, John Murray, 1964.

dahabiahs on leisurely voyages towards Nubia, the late 20th century has its advantages. Officials at Suez no longer get their drinking water by boat from India as they once did, and caviare comes by air. Though you will not sit cross-legged or dine off plate, the plumbing has much improved. If you can stomach the aseptic impersonality of skyscraper hotels, there are plenty of them, and Egyptian servants remain among the most courteous and efficient in the world. Communication is quick and easy; by plane you may range in a matter of hours from the Delta to the Sudan. The 20th century presents 5,000 years of history with a minimum of effort and trouble.

The rest depends, as it has always done, upon the taste and intelligence of the traveller. He can make or mar any landscape. A gentleman on his honeymoon once organized a vast display of fireworks for his bride in the temple of Karnak, and the lady-in-waiting to the Princess of Wales wrote in her diary: 'Saw another old temple, the name of which I am not certain.' Such persons might well stay nearer home. For others, every day in Egypt will bring experiences to be remembered; the country will imprint itself upon them, as it has done upon so many of their predecessors. The beauty of its landscape and the solemn perspective of its history will provoke their wonder, and their travellers' tales will not differ much from those that stirred the imagination of Bonaparte. Having watched the sun burn the mist off the Nile at dawn and heard the songs of the boatmen, having stood in the shadow of the Colossi of Memnon and walked in the mortuary temple of Hatshepsut, having seen twilight among the Tombs of the Caliphs and moonrise in the desert, the modern visitor, echoing an Englishman 350 years ago, may well exclaim, 'O soveraigne of streams, and most excellent of countries'.

1 A misty morning on the Nile. The efficient sail of the felucca resembles, as Ruskin noted, the shape of a swallow's wing.

2 Incised relief at Philae. The temples and the stories on the walls are a ledger of lost events and thoughts, betraying the secrets of changing generations and the beliefs of thirty dynasties.

3 The creaking of the *sakia,* whose wooden cogs are never oiled, seems like the complaint of the land and its people.

4 The *norag*: the traditional threshing machine.

5 Sun and shadow: an Egyptian village.

6 Village Elders: faces vaguely reminiscent of those on the walls of a thousand tombs.

7 The Nile flood from Nasser's gigantic storage tank has reached the water-carrier's bullock skin.

8 Bales of cotton, the gold of Egypt.

9 The flute-maker. Such crafts continue much as they have always done.

10 The potter remains the most talented and pleasing of the village craftsmen.

11 Children in a Coptic village, Upper Egypt.

12 Visiting the dead. Figures huddle beside the tombs in the buff, indeterminate desert.

13 Pyramids at Giza.

14 *Memento mori*: time and sand.

15 Fallen head of Rameses II, Thebes. The sun burns the broken and
prostrate god.

16 The god Horus portrayed as a falcon, Temple of Edfu. How should
the 20th century know the heart of Sekhmet the lion-goddess, or fear,
like Herodotus, even to pen the name of Osiris?

The Organized Oasis

Geography and climate can rarely have combined to produce a more unusual country. The roughly rectangular area that is Egypt, with the little appendage of Sinai, covers something over a million square kilometres; yet of this total no more than 3 to 4 per cent is green land. Cultivation is restricted to the entrenched and fertile Nile valley, and to the Delta, the lush triangle that lies between Cairo and the sea. From the first cataract at Aswan, down the valley to the apex of the Delta, is 450 miles; thence to the Mediterranean is another 100, while the coastal base of the Delta is a mere 150 miles wide. This green land, valley and Delta, whose shape has traditionally been compared to the stem and flower of the lotus, supports in crowded proximity a population rapidly approaching 40 million. By contrast, the deserts on either side that the ancients called the 'red' lands, to distinguish them from the dark nourishing silt of the cultivation, maintain on some 965,000 acres a mere 300,000 people.

It was not always so. The valley in early times was a jungle swamp and over much of the Delta, subsequently to be created by the deposits of the Nile, flowed the sea. The forebears of the Ancient Egyptians lived on the adjoining plateaux which were then savanna country, a grassy veld not unlike the uplands of East Africa and the home of elephant, lion, buffalo, zebra, and wild ass. On the fringes of what is now the Great Sand Sea, west of Cairo, lie

countless petrified trees that speak of vanished forest. There
followed a time of slow and relentless desiccation. The
uplands became desert, and the savanna peoples were
confronted with a grave challenge. They met it
triumphantly, venturing—no doubt initially with fear and
reluctance—into the dense Nile valley. Their ultimate
reward was Egyptian civilization. They gradually cleared,
drained, and cultivated both the valley and the emerging
Delta. By the 5th millennium they were building threshing
floors and granaries for their emmer wheat and barley, and
weaving crude linens; in the 4th millennium they were
fashioning shapely stone vases and decorated pottery,
mining gold and alabaster in the hills of the Eastern Desert,
and evolving a first primitive hieroglyphic writing. Somewhere about 3,000 B.C. valley and Delta were unified as a
single kingdom and the long history of the Dynasties
began.*

The nature of the kingdom was peculiar in that it had
many of the characteristics of an Oasis: the green fertility
was flanked by deserts, isolated from Nubia by the six
tumbling miles of the first Nile cataract, and separated
from the Mediterranean by a chain of lakes (Mareotis, Idkū,
Burullus, Manzala) and barely penetrable swamps. As late
as the 1st century A.D. the supply of hippopotami for the
games in Rome was still procured from the marshy fast-
nesses of the Delta. The country was also an oasis in the
sense that it was propitious to man. The date and dom
palm multiplied; flax, millet, lentils, leeks, onions, figs and
melons flourished; though the olive was never at home,
sesame seed and the castor plant produced oil; vines

* Dates for the Dynastic Period are those given in Hermann Kees's *Ancient Egypt:
A Cultural Topography* (1961), an invaluable work to which this chapter owes a
marked debt. A generation ago many Egyptologists ascribed dates several hundred
years earlier to the unification of the country and the Old Kingdom.

arrived in the 3rd millennium, perhaps from Syria or Cilicia, and viniculture so prospered that in the New Kingdom (*c.* 1568–1085) stoppered wine-jars sometimes carried particulars of vineyard, vintage, and the name of the *maître de chai*; though the horse and camel were late-comers, fine cattle (nobler beasts than the imported water-buffalo of modern Egypt), donkeys, pigs, goats, and sheep, were either indigenous or had arrived by dynastic times; the river yielded 190 species of fish, including the huge Nile perch, and the Delta lakes quantities of grey mullet; then as now the vast bird migrations passing through the Nile valley brought innumerable geese and duck, taken in nets or winged with throw-sticks. Only fine timber lacked; the native sycamore, acacia, and juniper produced an inferior wood. Trade soon was to supply even this want.

In the absence of rain, the economy depended on the beneficent Nile. The rainfall in Cairo is under two inches a year, and in Upper Egypt it is negligible. The river and its annual flood were the inexhaustible well that fed the oasis. The flood, product of torrential rain on the distant high-lands of Abyssinia, first reached Memphis about mid-June. The river continued to rise until mid-September, after which it gradually subsided. This timing was unique and providential. In Mesopotamia the Tigris and Euphrates delivered their flood-waters in the spring; crops sprouting as the flood subsided were inevitably parched in the heat of high summer, unless artificially irrigated. In the Nile valley, by contrast, the flood ebbed in late autumn, crops ripened naturally through the temperate winter, and came to harvest in early spring. Yet the Nile could be over-generous. Excessive floods swept away villages and devastated the valley. Control of the river, which involved a complex system of irrigation, water distribution, and eventually water rights, began in pre-dynastic times. It was soon to be associated with water conservation, equally essential in lean years when the flood proved inadequate. This taming of the Nile had social and political consequences of the first importance, for it necessitated co-operation, fostered a sense of community and led to that meticulous organization which was the characteristic strength of Ancient Egypt.

The Nile, as a means of communication, made a vital contribution to the unity of the oasis. Perhaps nowhere else in the Ancient World was transport so reliable and internal contact so easy. Here again fortune played a decisive role. Except during the khamsin, the fifty days in spring which bring dreaded sandstorms from the south, the prevalent wind from the Mediterranean blows steadily upstream, often for weeks at a time. Thus vessels can usually move with equal comfort upstream under sail or downstream on the current. The efficient and simple lateen sail, which resembles, as Ruskin noted, the shape of a swallow's wing, was in use from very early times. Fortunately too, in a country short of suitable timber, both boats and ropes could be fashioned from the abundant papyrus of the Delta.*

The oasis, so fertile, so well provided with internal communication, enjoyed secure frontiers. Until the camel reached Egypt some time in the 4th century B.C., the deserts presented a formidable barrier to invasion. As a precaution against the possible incursion of Beduin tribes, the pharaohs established posts in the nearer oases of the Western Desert (though the oasis of Siwa, lying beyond the

* Craft resembling small versions of ancient papyrus boats may still be seen on Lake Titicaca, where the Uri Indians of that treeless region build with the totora reed.

Great Sand Sea and fifteen days' travel from the Delta, was not occupied until almost the end of the Dynastic Period). In the Eastern Desert, where the Nile south of Qena was barely 100 miles from the Red Sea, the pharaohs had two good reasons for garrisoning the wells: first, they must deny them to a hostile force, and secondly they needed them to exploit the state goldmines in those waterless mountains. Along the Delta coast, lake and swamp provided as effective a defence as the sands further south. The only point of weakness was the bridge to Asia, the isthmus of Suez. Here defences were established as early as the Old Kingdom (c. 2676–2194), and much strengthened in the next millennium during the Imperial Age. As long as internal organization was effective, the Oasis state was hardly pregnable. Only twice in the 2,000 years that followed the unification of the kingdom were its defences seriously breached. On each occasion the invader, profiting from a period of internal dissension, crossed the isthmus of Suez.

In changing to their oasis habitat, the people of the adjoining plateaux did well for themselves. They came, as Herodotus says, to enjoy, 'the fruits of the field with less trouble than any other people in the world'; they were richer and more comfortable than their neighbours. Their circumstances, as we have seen, encouraged a sense of community and social values. In the three months' respite from agriculture that the Nile flood afforded, they had opportunity to undertake those ambitious communal works, the temples and tombs, that were monuments both to religion and to the pharaohs who acted as their representatives and intercessors with the gods. If a little unimaginative, the inhabitants of the valley and the Delta were kindly, sensible, and industrious in their pursuit of a well-regulated life. They looked on the happy side of things, appreciating their families, their orderly homes, and not least their gardens. Perhaps there was never a nation of such dedicated gardeners. If their enduring close-knit society, which must at times have seemed immutable, made them unduly conservative, they were the last to notice it. With little doubt as to the superiority of their own country and its customs, they regarded foreigners and their ways with habitual distaste.

When they deigned to look beyond their frontiers and to visit less fortunate peoples, it was to obtain those commodities—they were relatively few—that the abundance of their own valley failed to supply. The first and most important of these was timber. The nearest forests were those of the Lebanon and before the middle of the 3rd millennium they had set up a trading station at Byblos; thence during the 4th Dynasty a convoy of no less than forty vessels sailed on a single occasion with supplies of timber. It was the quest for timber that first made Mediterranean sailors of the Egyptians, and so large did the Lebanese trade loom in their minds that for 2,000 years sea-going vessels were known as 'Byblos-ships'. In due course Byblos became thoroughly Egyptianized, acquiring its temple and priesthood to serve a resident community of Nile merchants and officials. From further afield they obtained silver and, predominantly from Cyprus, copper: metals which were lacking in Egypt.

Later than the link with Byblos came trade missions down the Red Sea to Punt (probably to be identified as Somaliland), one of which is graphically depicted on the walls of Queen Hatshepsut's temple at Thebes. From Punt and Arabia the pharaohs acquired myrrh, balsam, pearls, ivory and cinnamon. It was to facilitate this trade that a canal linking the Delta and the Red Sea, started in the 26th Dynasty, was completed during the period of Persian rule in the 5th century (and restored by Ptolemy Philadelphus 200 years later). In Ptolemaic times, knowledge of the monsoons enabled vessels to reach India, freighting there with indigo, pepper, and silk. Payment for such imports, and the regular shipments of prized Lebanese cedar, presented no problem to a nation with rich gold deposits in the Eastern Desert, a monopoly of papyrus, a wealth of linen, and in later times a large exportable surplus of corn.

Against the foreground of European history, where a century or two span the rise and eclipse of great powers, the durability of the oasis civilization is a recurring source of wonder. It is the more astonishing in that the Egyptians were not a martial people. Their strength lay in organization and in their frontiers. In 2,500 years they seem to have fought only three major battles, and these were all in the last half of the 2nd millennium: Megiddo, Kadesh against the Hittites, and the decisive victory of Rameses III in the Delta against the Sea Peoples. On the whole the Egyptians had little regard for soldiers. Their esteem was reserved for administrators, civil servants, and craftsmen. Until the imperial adventures of the New Kingdom (c. 1568–1085), the Egyptians ventured abroad to trade rather than to conquer. Little beyond their frontiers offered charms to rival the relatively equable life of the Nile valley. Ironically it was the territorial ambitions of the pharaohs of the New Kingdom that ultimately contributed to the downfall of the state. Unable to recruit their pacific subjects in sufficient numbers, they relied increasingly on Syrian and Libyan mercenaries. When internal unity broke up at the end of the period, Libyans from the Western Desert, calling no doubt largely on their compatriots already settled in the Fayum, established a foreign dynasty.

The first unification of Egypt (*c*. 3000 B.C.), traditionally attributed to King Menes, was the achievement of the valley rather than the Delta, and it was repeatedly from the valley that the creative and organizing impulse was to come. Even today it is commonly said that the vitality of the country lies south of Cairo. By *c*. 2676 unification had led to the emergence of the powerful, highly integrated state known as the Old Kingdom, and Egyptian civilization had taken the form that was to persist so long unbroken. With its capital at Memphis, the Old Kingdom gave the world its first ashlar buildings at Sakkara and raised the vast pyramids of Giza. Its stability was unshaken for nearly 500 years, a period roughly as long as that which separates the Norman Conquest and the Armada.

The breakup came, as always in Egypt, with the weakening of central administration and the growth of provincial feudalism. Disunity enabled invaders to cross the isthmus of Suez, the kingdom was fragmented, and there followed the first Time of Troubles. In a country where the pendulum swings slowly, the troubles lasted for two centuries. Unity, when it returned, was imposed once again from the south. Society reassumed its characteristic Egyptian form, and the 12th and 13th Dynasties— pharoahs predominantly named Amenemhet and Sesostris— provided 300 years of stable rule, the period of the Middle Kingdom (1991–*c*. 1670).

The second Time of Troubles was precipitated not only by internal disunity but by a new weapon from Asia, the horse and war chariot, unfamiliar to the Egyptians. The mounted Hyksos swept over the isthmus and from *c*. 1700 to *c*. 1570 established a capital in the Delta. Once more unity was eventually restored from the south, and the traditional pattern was re-established with the New Kingdom. Like the Old Kingdom, it lasted some 500 years (*c*. 1568–1085) and its familiar memorials are the tombs and temples of Thebes. It also saw the imperial phase of Egyptian history, when pharaohs such as Thutmosis III and Rameses II extended their rule to the Euphrates. The wealth and apparent stability of Nile civilization was never greater than in this period, but the mould, which contrary to all historical precedent had already lasted some two millennia, was weakening. Cohesion was lost under the last Rameside pharaohs, and in the 10th century the Libyans came to rule over Egypt.

Though the forms of the ancient civilization persisted, bulwarked by the conservatism of the people and the prestige conferred by so long and splendid a past, Egypt thenceforward was the prize of foreigners. Ethiopians, Assyrians, Persians contended for the kingdom of the pharaohs. In the 4th century B.C. the last native ruler of Egypt, Nectanebos II, abandoned hope and fled southward. Soon after, in 332, Alexander the Great arrived. The Egypt of the Ptolemies, of Christiantity, and of Islam, were to be something very different. They have left their imposing memorials in Alexandria, in the monasteries of the desert, and in the dusty glitter of medieval Cairo.*

By the time the country made its first contact with the modern world, in the guise of Bonaparte and his troops, Ancient Egypt had long been no more than legend. The progressive rediscovery of pharaonic civilization over the next 150 years is one of the outstanding achievements of archaeology. If the Egyptians owe any debt to Europe it is to Denon, Belzoni, Champollion, Lepsius, and their successors. Yet in

* See Chapters 8–10.

a sense a quintessence of the past has always survived, for the unchanged landscape is that of Ancient Egypt and, in spite of the lapse of centuries, the peasants of the valley, the fellahin, are representative of the race of the pharaohs and share not a few of their virtues.

———————◆◆◆◆◆————————

THREE

The Valley Landscape

Through an inclement desert, treeless and unwatered, the Nile has carved its passage. In so doing it has created the landscape of Egypt. Between barren hills a belt of green, narrowing or widening with the valley, faithfully pursues the course of the river. Though it expands below Cairo into the fan-shaped Delta, this luxuriant strip, sandwiched between the arid and the uninhabitable, is the essential land of Egypt. It sometimes seems such chance: this green wedged fortuitously between an eternity of sand might easily not have been. Yet it is so reasonable: one sees clearly how it came to exist. Looking down from the desert, you may seize the country in a glance: a single view explains the landscape of Egypt.

In the midst moves the slow river, with two or three white sails catching the sunlight. Alluvial and patient, the fields on either side receive its waters. From the main stream the canals diverge like arteries and go about their duties. From these again spread the lesser veins, and at last, glinting under the sun, trickle the separate rivulets that the water-wheels raise to souse a single field or a few square yards of land.

All this water moves by devious ways through a versatile patchwork of greens, doubly lush by contrast to the adjacent desert, and variegated with yellow maize stalks, or purple-

brown earth where a crop has not yet sprung. Scattered
forests of date palms and clumps of sycamore seem like the
precise and miniature trees on a geographical model. Little
mud roads, raised above the level of the fields, run purposefully up and down: dropped in the belt of green at decent
intervals are dun mud villages, differentiated sometimes by
a minaret or the whitewashed front of a headman's house.
In this 450 miles of landscape the towns, though sometimes
little more than vastly swollen villages, seem oddly
anomalous, and the railway runs with an embarrassed air.
The water, the unhedged field, the palm, and the village are
the essence.

Across this scene for six winter months the sun moves in
absolute and continuous clemency. This is the season when
the ancients thought that the sun-god Ra in his heavenly
boat performed his duties with the greatest consideration,
neither scorching the crops, nor allowing too much licence
to the north wind. Rising from the Eastern Desert the sun
sips up the heavy winter dews and passes daily across the
valley through a cloudless sky. At evening it sinks behind
the Libyan hills, creating, as a magnificent finale, its breath-
catching sunsets. Day after day the progress is repeated;
day after day the evolution is the same. Looking out over
the valley, you realize that this changelessness is central to
the scene, that the constancy of the sun is reflected in the
permanence of the landscape, and that the latter alters
little from generation to generation, or from century to
century. The very soil of Egypt has a quality of persistence,
seeming to resist innovation. The pattern of the cultivation,
the group of palms, the squat village, the mud road, are
perennial. In spite of the new electric pylons, the valley
that stretches below you is that of the pharaohs, and Ancient
Egypt lies there, preserved in the balsam of the sun and the

conservative instincts of the inhabitants. Here has been throughout later history no change in rainfall, no forests grown or felled, and no enclosure movement hedging the land; few new roads have sliced across the fields, and even today industry leaves them largely unscarred. The Ancient Egyptian returning in 2000 B.C. from goldmines in the Red Sea desert saw this cultivated strip, and Arab caravans plodding to the valley brink were gladdened by the same water and the same white sails.

Nile, soil, and sun provide the permanent basis of the scene, its raw material; and the fellah organizes it, contributing a flavour that makes it yet more Egyptian. His is the patchwork quilt of crops, and his the character of the village. His, too, that essential feature of the Egyptian landscape, its human animation. Those little figures that appear to move soundlessly in the valley below are a more integral part of the scene than are the inhabitants of any Western countryside. In the fields no composition is complete without man and beast: the child on the Indian buffalo; the family asleep under the banyan tree, with camel and donkey ruminating beside them; half-naked figures bent over the soil; and the man raising water. With a dense population, 60 per cent of whom are dependent on agriculture, the interaction of man and nature is close. The Egyptian scene is inescapably human; there are always figures absorbed in the simple processes of agricultural life. The cultivation has little of that romantic appeal which is associated in Europe with the countryside. These ploughed and reploughed acres have nothing to do with copses, blackthorn thickets, dells and heaths; wild flowers cannot find a square foot alongside the crops. Here is no wildness, no communion with solitude, but a limited amount of fertile land carefully organized to support a dense population.

Yet this alluvial plotted landscape is one of the most satisfying in the world. This satisfaction relates to its subtlety. The Egyptian scene, neither obvious nor sentimental, has often a rare aesthetic appeal; something of the quality of abstract art derives from its infinite variations of shape, colour and tone. The composition of the patchwork quilt, the perspective of road and canal, the third dimension of the palms, and not least the quality of the light, combine to produce effects of extraordinary delicacy. Only in the direct midday sun does the composition lose significance for an hour or two. The broads of East Anglia are the comparison which may spring to mind. There is the same wide sky, the same canals, the same clump of trees posed gracefully in the middle distance. But while in Egypt you miss the magnificent pile of clouds towering over the horizon which is essential to the East Anglian scene, you receive the impression of a landscape less weighted, more various and delicate. Egypt has the form of East Anglian country with the light and tone of Provence.

For those who react favourably to heather in flower against a blue sky, this Egypt is meaningless, except perhaps at sunset. Then for an hour or so the scene changes to turquoise, viridian, mauve and gold. Sometimes the colours create stupendous effects, but more often achieve the Egypt of the postcard: the gleam of water, the silhouetted pyramid, and palms dramatic against a flamboyant sky. This is the romantic *tour de force* which the subtlety of the Egyptian landscape for ten hours a day can afford to disdain.

From Aswan to Alexandria the same interplay of colours and shapes is endlessly repeated under the lucent sunlight of Egypt. Yet repetition is achieved without monotony. Tone and line are in constant though barely perceptible change, and from time to time occur those more obvious variations of theme, where for instance the purple sugar-canes of Upper Egypt are replaced by the cotton-fields of the Delta.

From a Nile boat the intimate changes of this landscape, together with the human animation which is so integral a part of it, are best savoured. Swallow-winged feluccas drop past with bales of cotton, sugar-cane, or earthenware pots, and bronze men in loin-cloths swing their nets from small rocking boats. Along the banks pass, as in a frieze, the dwellers in the fields: the women with their magnificent carriage, bearing pots or bundles on their heads; the peasant with his hoe; the swaying camel loaded with a mountain of clover; the patient long-eared ass; and the trailing children in charge of beasts ten times their size. And always there are the crops and beyond the distant clumps of palms.

As you slip downstream, hour by hour and day by day, the picture seems to have neither beginning nor end. The frieze along the banks is infinitely repeated. The child on the buffalo, the man laboriously raising water, you have seen a hundred times. You have seen that white egret probing the river mud, and long since put up those red-shanks from the spit beside the rushes. In the evening you have heard the boatmen sing the same songs, and you have seen the same palms silhouetted against a crimson sky. And always observing the river there has been that line of desert hills, now white and colourless, now sandy-grey, now mauve or pink at sunset. Sometimes they seem to oppress the valley in their featureless aridity; sometimes they seem kindly, protective, giving point and compactness to the scene. But they are always present, always repeated, always, like everything in the Egyptian landscape, suitable and inevitable. At last you may come to think that your boat has never moved, that your progress was illusion, and that you have but watched the infinitely varied play of light and colour on a single landscape.

Built of Nile mud, the villages are a continuation of the fields in different shape. It is hard to say where the village begins or ends, what is sun-baked soil and what is sun-baked wall. When a house falls, as it often does (for the Egyptian is slow to repair), it is earth lapsing to earth again. This close connection between soil and village reflects the relation of the landscape to the fellah himself. They are complementary, and as one watches their inter-action throughout the day the significance of each becomes clearer.

At dawn the landscape wakes, the mist stirs over a canal, palms take shape, and in silence the cultivation gains colour. Though beautiful, this is a modified and static fulfilment. The human animation and the movement are missing, there are no figures bending over the crops, and the scene is not Egypt. High in the sky only the flighting teal are moving. Not until the sun has risen does the land-scape become the fellah's again, and only in his presence does it attain its natural equilibrium. From every village on camel, on donkey, on foot, in pairs, in families, in groups, men, women and children troop out to their field-work. With them go their provisions and their tools. On narrow paths man jostles beast; they talk and their jokes break the morning silence. As the procession moves on, it thins; each acre claims its man and family. Soon the paths are empty again and the familiar figures are bent over the familiar soil. Now the houses, that held not only people—three and five to a room—but beasts packed in close proximity, are half-empty. The morning exodus has stripped the village. Only the old and idlers remain. You realize

that the real life of these people is not in the village at all
but in the fields. They sleep in their houses; but they live
among their crops.

The sun rises higher and they dispose soil and water in
their immemorial ways. One turns up his acre with the
plough of the pharaohs, while behind him following the
furrow, as we see on the wall-paintings of Sakkara, step
neat white egrets. One labouring at his *shadūf* raises a
stream of rich water to rich soil. It explores its way down
a maze of runnels that hand and hoe have cleared. Near by
a donkey stands expecting orders, as they always seem to
do. Beyond, there are men and women among the tall
maize stalks. They are gathering the ears; you can hear their
voices, but only their heads appear. By the edge of the
canal men are transporting soil. Two of them are in long
galabiyehs of faded ultramarine, and the baskets on their
heads are identical with those in which their forefathers
carried soil for the pharaohs of the 12th Dynasty. On the
edge of the palm grove, high up under a tuft of fronds,
something white is moving. A loin-cloth. The man slung
round the trunk of the palm has been gathering dates all
the morning; his wife takes them as they are lowered. Under
a great banyan tree in the middle of a field two children are
playing and beside them their tethered buffalo crops a clean
circle in the berseem clover.

When you look again all action has ceased. The water
stands in the furrows, the white egrets are motionless,
nothing agitates the green maize leaves. You are aware of
the hum of insects. The sun is high and there are no
shadows. The people are sleeping. They have eaten
unleavened bread or rice, and have stretched out among the
crops. They lie in every field and by every canal. They seem
to have fallen without forethought, in any place and with

c

their implements around them. Some have handkerchiefs over their faces; some lift a vague arm from time to time as though to drive away the flies. The children under the tree are sleeping with heads tucked into their elbows, and even the donkey after hesitation has lowered itself laboriously to the ground and dozes. Only the camel, kneeling sphinx-like, refuses to close an eye, and from time to time turns a supercilious head towards the sleepers.

Time passes; and in a daily resurrection all awake and rise, man and beast. The hand takes up the hoe; the donkey staggers to its feet; the buffalo submits to the plough; voices again drown the hum of insects and a wheel begins to creak, raising water. So it goes on until evening, figure and action inextricably interwoven with the landscape. Then as the sun settles on the desert, a new light floods the scene, oblique, dramatic, highly coloured. Sometimes in garish ostentation, sometimes in true pharaonic magnificence, the sun goes down. As a new lighting in an instant transforms the setting of a stage, so the landscape now is changed and the varied cast departs. This is no longer their scene. Calling their children, untethering the beasts, loading themselves and their ploughs upon the asses' backs, the fellahin straggle home along the canal to the village. Swallows flick the water, and a cloud of midges wavers on the air. An old black ferry-boat, down to the gunnels, loaded indifferently with men and animals, creeps across to the farther bank. A group of plum-purple Indian buffalo slip one by one into the water behind, seeming suddenly not the docile tractors that they are but primitive, amphibious monsters.

So all are gathered into the compact circle of the village, where, under the lamps, field and desert are shut out. Huge fruit-bats twist now in a lame unpeopled landscape, the night heron flaps from its daylight shelter, and from the desert a fox comes down to water. The heavy Egyptian dew begins to fall. Seated in the darkness by his fire the field watchman pulls round his shoulders a long cloak of camel's hair or an old army greatcoat, and is alone until dawn.

Such is the time-table of the day and the landscape. Details are filled in later: the tameness of the birds, and near or far the mellifluous fluting of the palm dove; the good manners of the sand-coloured dogs; the absence of wild flowers; patterns made by bare feet on wet or dusty paths; splashes of colour, like the happy juxtaposition of faded blue *galabiyehs* and the yellow of dead maize stalks; and the ever-recurring sound, somewhere out in the fields, of a pipe and people, often children, singing. On closer acquaintance palms acquire unsuspected character. One notices that in the distance they are the greyish-green of olive trees, that doves delight in them, and that one can never reach the centre of a palm grove and the green gloom that one expects to find there. The trees with their graceful leaning trunks stand easily apart and are always threaded with light, so that it is no darker, no more secluded, in the heart of the grove than on its wavy edge.

The palm in Egypt is not the symbol of peace, but of labour. For the fellahin the whole landscape symbolizes work. The monotonous regularity of their lives reflects their land-bound overlorded history, and the black garments of the women, so pleasing visually, seem like a perpetual mourning. The oxen that turn the innumerable *sakias* lifting the water from the Nile are blindfold; they, like their owners, plod on year by year, approaching no goal but death, and unconscious of their vital importance in the agricultural scheme. All through the fields you hear the creaking of these *sakias,* whose wooden cogs are never oiled. The notes may differ but the sound is always present, hanging over the river, creeping across the crops. This perpetual sighing, helpless and hopeless, comes to seem like the complaint of the land and its people. The dirge is inescapable.

FOUR

The Dwellers on the Land

On the lush green of the cultivation the villages of Egypt appear to have been thrown up long ago like molehills. There are said to be 4,000 of them. Densely populated, many contain 2,000 or 3,000 people, but in a country where land is so valuable few villages straggle. They tend to be compact; the assiduously laboured fields lap like a green wave against adobe walls. Raised above the level of the surrounding country by the accretions and dilapidations of centuries, and each with its attendant palm grove, the villages were seen at their best in the old days when the Nile inundated the land in Upper Egypt to the depth of a foot or two and they rose like populous palm-fringed islands. A closer impression is less favourable. They are earthy and of the earth. The jumbled honeycomb of huts, where it is hard to differentiate between the dwellings of men and beasts, sometimes seem like the product of instinct, and not the conscious and pondered construction of men.

The houses, simple hovels most of them, are of hard sun-dried mud, bricked up into walls. Within, the floors and the raised quarter of the room where they sleep are also beaten earth, and so is the bench or mastaba built against the wall outside the doorway. Somewhere, either in the house or in the small courtyard behind, there will be a mud-brick oven. Set in a maze of lanes and paths, these dwellings huddle together. Here in all seasons the sun beats down, drying, desiccating, crumbling the walls, and thickening the dust on the ground. A house cracks up and trickles away, and the same soil, patted afresh into newer bricks, will rise again. The air is heavy with motes; shoulder rubs shoulder. This is the warren in which each generation repeats its predecessor with exactitude. Here since the beginning of history they have been born, married, and buried with ceremony.

Strangely, the drab scene has much to offer. A village on a canal nearly always makes its point; and in most villages there is detail not easily forgotten: a sycamore tree draped over the modest dome of a sheikh's tomb, a scattering of pigeons into a clear sky from one of the ample dovecots which nearly every community supports, a whitewashed façade as a backcloth for moving figures, a group of women posed on the river bank. The two-storeyed house of the *omdah*, or village headman, and perhaps those of one or two richer peasants, add architectural variety. So does the modest mosque, often with a minaret, from which five times a day the muezzin, usually a blind man, calls to prayer. Such ritual strikes the observer as strange in this agglomeration of mud huts, and it hints at complexities which sun-baked bricks do not at first suggest.

Evening is kindest to the village. Shapes are blurred; dust disappears with the failing light. Crowding the narrow streets the fellahin and their beasts come in from the fields: the dry warren pulses with an accelerated life. The mastabas set against the house-fronts, empty at noon, are now the nuclei of little groups that talk, or argue, or stare lazily about them, tired at the day's end. Cross-legged in his doorway a tailor sews in the half-light, as though by touch; the village barber, seated like his customer on the ground, finishes off a day's work; and the itinerant vendors, hawking bric-à-brac, cotton goods and vegetables, circulate with their throaty cries. By contrast the women go unobtrusively about their affairs, and standing within doorways seem to shun the light. Their full black dresses and the black shawls over their heads melt easily into the growing darkness.

In the coffee-house the lamp is lit, or now increasingly the electricity. The rush-bottomed chairs are filled, hookahs are handed round and small cups of Turkish coffee. The gathering is a purely male rite, and the bright light accentuates the importance of all that happens there. Gestures take on a dramatic flavour, the story-teller's face holds the eye, and a roar of laughter batters its way out between the huts to the deserted crops. Though the wardrobe of the cast is modest, this is a traditional and ancient stage. Most of the characters appear in a simple *galabiyeh*, a long cotton garment, blue, striped, or white, with full sleeves and low-cut neck. Their feet may well be bare, and on their heads many wear a skull-cap, around which some have twisted the narrow, white, Muslim turban. Those who have had contact with the towns wear in addition a three-quarter length European topcoat over their *galabiyehs*. But it is the old sheikh in heavy silk caftan and coloured sash, with spotless turban, who steals the show. It takes considerable estate to support such silk.

The stranger as he scans these faces finds something vaguely reminiscent. Then it dawns on him that the old lips pursed uncommunicatively round the stem of a pipe, the young man in profile against the light, are from Ancient Egypt. These faces have their duplicates, perhaps their more convincing replicas, on the walls of a thousand dark tombs. Here in the coffee-house are pharaonic people.

Someone pushes back a chair and looks into the street. Isolated for a moment the type emerges yet more clearly. The smooth forehead, the low-bridged nose, the thick long eyelashes, the prominent cheekbones, and an almost feminine delicacy: these are familiar. So, too, is the body, well assembled and a little below medium height, yet looking shorter by reason of the flat splayed feet which are cracked and fissured by days spent in saturated fields. Even the *galabiyeh* dates from the 6th Dynasty. Here is none of the heaviness of the Negro; no superfluous energy or swelling muscle, but the economy, the spare efficiency, of the figures labouring on the walls of tombs. There is little beauty here in the commonly accepted sense, none of that glowing health popularly associated with a peasantry. There is, on the other hand, a suitableness of part to part, a proportion such as few peoples are endowed with. The European underrates the looks of the fellahin. The women, with matted hair and faces that by twenty-five life has scored, have few sentimental attractions. Yet they keep a magnificent carriage into old age and have finer hands than Westerners.

Certain traits of character have come down unchanged through centuries, and the curious contrasts of good and bad that make up the contemporary fellah have their ancient parallels. Thus those domestic virtues which one senses in the Egyptian life of the golden 12th Dynasty, before the country developed imperial ambitions, have descended to the fellah. 'To please your father is to please God,' says Muhammad; happy family relationships, devotion to, and affection from, children, are a salient feature of village life. At the same time the fellah shares the obstinate conservatism and provincialism of the Ancient Egyptian. He is still prepared to believe that all rivers must flow north as does

the Nile; and, like his ancestors, might well refer to the
Euphrates as 'that inverted flood which goes downstream
in going upstream'. He has inherited that lack of intellectual
curiosity which was so marked a feature of the civilization
of the Nile. Like his predecessors the fellah rarely uses his
mind except for practical ends. In spite of his cunning, his
ready wit, and his long memory, impractical speculation
rarely disturbs his thoughts. Another legacy from the
distant past, though it may owe something also to Islam,
is his ritualistic courtesy and politeness which seem the
vestiges of some elaborate code of social behaviour such
as might develop in a great state. Egyptian courtesy has
always been renowned, and (off the tourist beat) the stranger
will find consideration and tact springing like flowers from
mud and toil. These virtues, like the fellah's hospitality, his
lack of snobbery, and his ease in the presence of the rich,
are attractive qualities. The peasant, inviting you without
hesitation to take coffee with him, remains altogether
unimpressed by social status and class distinction. In the
Turk he once acknowledged a master, but not a superior;
though he may have been afraid, he was not impressed.
Today he meets the rich and powerful without embarrass-
ment; the gulf that separates them he rightly realizes is
usually one of circumstance. This lack of social subservience
is symbolized in the code of greeting that prevails. The
greater must always greet the less: thus the horseman
greets the rider on the donkey, the latter greets the man on
foot, and he greets the woman; so the welcome runs on and
goes at last from the child to the beast.

The routine of the fellah's life and the minute circle of his
horizon, which did not until recently allow him to glimpse
a different or more prosperous condition, contribute to
another element of his character, his constant cheerfulness.

The very constriction of his world makes possible his ready smile. His own pleasures and possessions are all he knows: his God, his children, his women, his crops. Beyond the village fields lies the unknown. This little world, almost as limited as a child's, is reflected in childlike qualities, his jokes and sudden irrepressible gaiety passing as suddenly into anger and rage. The fellah's crimes are those of the child, done in the heat of uncontrolled passion and repented an hour later.

It is the small circle of his environment which, less happily, generates those personal animosities, often as irrational as schoolboy feuds, that affect village life, and that on a wider scale are sometimes reflected in violent inter-village quarrels. The same limited orbit, the circumscription of the fellah's vision, also concentrates his energies upon a single activity, that of raising and selling crops, and impresses two objectives upon him: the acquisition of land and of money. To this everything may become subservient.

The personality that we have indicated, courteous, cheerful, quick, and strongly acquisitive, does not accord with the role played by the fellahin throughout history. In spite of conservative instincts and an unreliable temper, such a people would appear made for success; sons of mammon, they should have been predators. Yet for 5,000 years they have remained tillers of the soil. There is an ingredient in the compound, and an important one, that we have not yet mentioned: the Egyptian in spite of his positive qualities is characterized by passivity. He will bear the greatest calamities with the greatest indifference, and collectively his meek endurance in the face of imposition and oppression is a matter of history. He invented fatalism long before Islam. This passivity leads to lack of drive; the fellah rarely moulds or organizes, and the force of his personality is imprinted chiefly on his landscape.

The age-long passivity of the fellah is said to relate to his religious temperament, his health, and the unpredictability of the Nile flood. Herodotus, most observant of travellers, noted that the Egyptians were 'religious to excess, far beyond any other race of men'. The religious zeal which he noted has never left the Nile valley, nor has its character altogether changed. Whether the disciple of Ra, Christ, or Muhammad, the Egyptian has been ritualistic rather than active in his faith. The incantational, magical formulae of religion have always played a great part in his beliefs, as has an excessive preoccupation with the next world. For the Ancient Egyptian an exact and trivial formula was his only passport through the hall of the judging gods; for his Muslim descendant salvation lies with similar arbitrariness in the gift of Allah. Moral exertion and his energies on earth count for little. He has lain in the lap of the gods, and in the end has been content to lie there.

As for health, a high percentage of fellahin suffer from a sinister and endemic disease, bilharzia. Its effects have been found in mummies of the 12th Dynasty, and thus the people have been subject to this scourge for 4,000 years. Bilharzia does not reveal its ravages to the statistician of mortalities. It works in a more subtle and noxious way, affecting the character of those whom it attacks. The germ, that lives upon a little snail in the stagnant water of the canals and fields where the fellah is obliged to work, carries with it inertia and lassitude. Modern methods of irrigation, calculated to produce bigger crops at the expense of a people's health, have increased the spread of the disease. Only recently have the authorities begun seriously to grapple with it. If modern methods and medicine can eliminate the germ, they may dramatically modify the character of the fellah. The possibility is epic and might create a changed people. We have some idea what they would be like: the *Saidi* in certain parts of Upper Egypt, where the incidence of bilharzia is relatively low, are a byword for strength and vigour.

It is said that a people, growing up in the valley of a great river and dependent for life and livelihood on the caprice of floods over which they have no control, develop passivity. They cannot modify the forces of nature which bring plenty or famine; their life is arbitrary and crops are given or withheld through no virtue or vice of their own. When effort and planning serve no purpose, a people can only face events with apathy and learn to suffer cataclysms without a murmur. So it was for millennia in Egypt. But now the Nile is predictable.

The monster Nasser Dam at Aswan has tamed the river. Whatever its disastrous side-effects, and they are probably many, the fellah no longer lives at the caprice of floods. His world has grown more rational. In time he will discover that forethought and enterprise have a new value. Passivity will be out of date.

While awaiting the slow effects of change, the fellah remains the same complex of kindness, gaiety, quick wit, anger, and apathetic docility that he was in pharaonic times. He also retains his native idiosyncrasies and customs. Many of these, such as the long braids of false hair, falling to the waist, that women sometimes wear, or the cicatrized incisions on cheekbones, once probably tribal marks, are understandable enough. Again, a non-bigamous plurality of wives, or the brutal treatment of unchaste girls, though strange to our thinking, are based on a recognizable process of thought. The fellah would be able to advance reasons for these practices which might appear relevant.

But there is a side of the fellah's life which reflects a world hardly comprehensible to us. It is, with increasing education, a shrinking world, but none the less there are times when a curtain drops and the landmarks of reason and logic are gone. The mud village, as though its worldly struggles were not enough, is subject to the jinn. These capricious tyrannical people, though living below ground in an organized society of their own, lend themselves readily to the evil practices of those who wish others harm. At all costs the jinn must not be antagonized. Since they are made of flame, and love their native element, before anything is thrown into the fire the fellah must be careful to say aloud, 'In the name of Allah, the Compassionate, the Merciful,' thus giving the jinn due warning. Similarly care must be taken not to wet a jinn, and before pouring water on the ground one must cry, 'Permission, O blessed ones.' In addition to the jinn the village supports another army of shadowy and often malevolent people, for every fellah has his ghostly double. This spirit, which recalls the *ka* of the Ancient Egyptians, is born and dies with its earthly fellow. Jealousy is a salient feature of these barren spirits and their efforts to harm or entice away the children of their living doubles cause the fellahin endless anxiety.

In this world of fantasy the magician and the spellbinder inevitably play a part. They are the fellah's allies who can counteract the forces of the unseen and the evil eye of his fellows. Until recent years they were much in demand. Their help was sought in every dilemma, and their charms and incantations paid for. The love-philtre, the rigmarole that will bring health, the symbolism that will injure an enemy, these were the recourse of every village. To induce fertility women would walk seven times round the Great Pyramid, or journey to Cairo to touch a certain mummy in the

Museum. Men were tattooed to cure bad eyesight or the toothache. Everywhere and at all hours moved the evil eye, which with infinite expenditure of labour the fellah hoped to combat. With meticulous care he collected and burnt nail-parings and hair-combings, for through these an enemy might gain disastrous power over him. Even today over the door of his house he sometimes hangs in fear a little plate, or the horns of a sheep; his wife wears a charmed necklace of light blue beads and allows her long black dress to trail in the dust, thus obliterating her footsteps. Naturally it is the fellah's most precious possession, his children, which are most exposed to the evil eye and the agency of jinn. They need elaborate protection. Since a son is the fellah's first wish, and hence runs the greatest danger, he has been known to circumvent the evil eye by disguising a male infant as a girl for a year or two. But girls or boys must, with indiscriminate care, be hedged with charms. From the first moment of pregnancy the fellah's magic must guard his child. Incantations greet its birth and the infant sometimes starts on its long agricultural life with a piece of umbilical cord round its neck, tied appropriately enough in a piece of cotton. This chess-play of charm and countercharm, this fantastic world of ghosts and fears, may lie within a few hundred yards of an electric pumping station, or within sight of the lighted windows of the wagons-lits that glide the sleeping tourist to Luxor.

FIVE

Life in the Village

The word 'fellah' means 'one who tills', and the Egyptian peasant lives up to his name. The land is his life. Poor, and sometimes hungry, he issues smiling to the fields. Since the successful agrarian reforms of the 1950s, and the expropriation of large estates, these fields are often his own. When they are not, legislation controls the tenant-rent he will have to pay. Yet the holdings are often pitiably small, for the population has doubled in the last forty years and the pressure on land is intense. In his day Muhammad 'Ali was able to grant each honest fellah three acres of land. Before the end of the 19th century, the acreage *per capita,* with the increase in population, was down to 0·65. Twenty years later, in spite of extensive land reclamation and large new areas under the plough, the population had further increased in relation to the acreage. The figure was 0·42 acres per person, less than in Japan. In an industrial society this ratio might not have been significant, but in agricultural Egypt it meant everything. Even today when the Nasser Dam has brought nearly 1¼ million additional acres under cultivation, and 2½ million peasants (including families) have been settled on the new land, the pressure continues to grow inexorably. The population is increasing at the rate of a million a year.

Though expropriation for debt and the accursed moneylender are things of the past, and though both the Ottoman knout and forced labour on the canals have faded from memory, the fellah has few expectations. Even with modern irrigation, the natural owners of the richest soil in the world remain desperately poor. It is a situation to which centuries have accustomed them. Most peasants make a pittance. There is rarely a surplus to put aside; the economic vice is tight.

In such conditions the fellah carries on, apparently heedless of all that happens around him. He works much as in the past, with tools hardly changed and with methods that often prove more efficient and more suited to the country than the scientific procedures which have recently been introduced, more particularly in the newly reclaimed lands. The humble ass was with him from the beginning. The Hyksos invaders, the Shepherd Kings, brought the horse, and not long before the coming of Christ he acquired the camel. Archimedes gave him the baffling screw which, turned by hand, raises the water of the Nile. The *sakia* and *shadūf*, the commonest water-lifters, are both pharaonic in origin. The *sakia* is the creaking, groaning wheel, turned by blindfold oxen, to which we have referred. The *shadūf* consists of a leather bucket attached to a long wooden bar with a counterweight; this bar pivots on a wooden support, and as the bucket is dipped and raised it brings up the Nile water. Working the *shadūf* is, the fellahin claim, laborious, and as they water their land they sing a song symbolic of their labour:

> Hast thou resolved upon strangling me, O God?
> Loosen the noose!
> No mother weeps for me, no aunt, no sister.

Most of his other implements—his wooden plough, with iron-tipped share, his hoe, which replaces a spade in the

Nile valley, and his *maktaf*, the wicker basket in which he carries soil—also have their origins in the distant past. In processes such as threshing and winnowing, the same persistence can be traced. When his corn, cut with a simple hand-sickle, has been gathered, the threshing is accomplished by driving a curious wooden cart, with a serried row of sharp-edged iron discs set side by side, round and round over the outspread sheaves. The heavy discs break up the corn and detach the grain from husk and stalk. The grain is then ready for winnowing. This is achieved by the rudimentary process of throwing it into the air with a wooden fork, identical in form and construction with the forks used for the same purpose on the threshing-floors of the pharaohs. The grain falls straight to the ground; the lighter chaff is wafted off by the north wind that day after day blows up the valley. The fellah is tenaciously conservative, but he did not arrive at his present methods without a long period of trial and error in a distant past. His traditional way of doing things often turns out best. It is significant that he often stubbornly, but usually rightly, prefers a mud-brick dwelling built at little cost to expensive new housing built in concrete. Mud-brick he knows is warmer in winter and cooler in summer than the alternative which progress supplies.

But in one way progress has profoundly changed the fellah's life. A regular water-supply has revolutionized his farming. The history of Egypt has always been linked to the supply of water; at all times good canals and an equable distribution of water have meant relative prosperity. When we read in the past of famine, poverty, or misrule, we find the ancient scribe complaining that the waterways have been allowed to silt up, that there is weed in the canals, and that the crops are dying of thirst. It is difficult to conceive the amount of water in tons which is needed to mature a crop under the hot summer sun of Egypt. The total rainfall demanded by a crop in the temperate English climate would suffice a field of cotton for a bare three weeks in the Egyptian summer. In a period of great heat such a crop demands something like twenty tons per acre per day.

The Nile flood was always first perceptible in Cairo in late June and the arrival of the flood-water was once the occasion for a human, and later for a token, sacrifice. The river continued to rise rapidly throughout the summer and attained its maximum in the autumn. From October onwards it slowly decreased in volume, until the following spring when it reached its lowest level. The rich flood-silt in the course of a century added four inches of Abyssinian soil to the Nile valley. Hence its immense fertility.

In late summer and autumn the nourishing flood more than sufficed the needs of the country, and quantities of unused water poured out to sea and to waste. From ancient times it was realized that the problem of irrigation would be largely solved if this vast surplus could be stored for use in spring and early summer: to this end the pharaohs apparently used Lake Karun in the Fayum with some success. But it was only with the creation of the Nasser Dam, completed in 1968, that the flood was fully controlled. This huge dyke, towering over the Nile valley not far above the point where the river is precipitated down the first cataract, conserves the flood-waters, creating a reservoir 500 kilometres long and ten kilometres wide that extends beyond the frontiers of the Sudan. The sluices of this gigantic storage tank now methodically release the flood-waters as they are needed and crops are impartially irrigated throughout the year. Thus the land is never out of use, and for twelve months the fellah can expect a modicum of water. This is in direct contrast to the old basin irrigation, less productive but more healthy and more picturesque, by which vast areas were inundated at the Nile flood and the fellah, Noah-like, planted his crop as the soil emerged from beneath the ebbing waters. So completely is the flood now utilized, together with the normal Nile flow, that in early summer practically no water escapes to the sea, except the 'dead' water which drains off the land after use. Indeed, the Egyptians have long found it necessary to build temporary barrages at Rosetta and Damietta to prevent sea-water flowing back into the empty mouths of the Nile. The side-effects of the Nasser Dam are less happy. Most of the rich silt is now deposited in the great lake above the dam, and the perennial irrigation of the Nile valley has danger-ously raised the water-table. The ambitious undertaking may in the long term prove disastrous.

Meanwhile, the regulated flood reaches the cultivation mainly by 'free flow'. This means that the water is not generally raised to the fields by electric turbines or similar means, but is held up by a series of barrages often 100 miles above the districts where it will be used. From these barrages it is conveyed by canal at a leisurely pace, and at a higher level than the Nile, until finally it is released to flow freely into the areas which it must irrigate.

Perennial irrigation and the infinitely larger quantity of water now captured make possible two and three crops a year, and not least the extensive cottonfields of the Delta. Cotton in tree-form was known to the pharaohs, but the cotton-plant proper came with Muhammad 'Ali. Today Egypt, with the help not only of her climate but of the cheap labour available for constant hoeing, has evolved perhaps the finest cotton in the world. On this depends much of the country's wealth, and an annual income in recent years of some 400 million dollars. Though once the granary of the Roman Empire, her wheat is as bad in quality as her cotton is good, so the fellah often prefers to feed himself and his family on lentils or maize, the last a quicker-ripening crop introduced in the last century. Berseem, the ubiquitous local clover, fulfils a double purpose: it is excellent fodder and at the same time a great fertilizer by its nitrogen-creating properties. So rich is the soil and so propitious the sun that this clover will often yield from fifty to sixty tons per acre over a period of a few months. Other crops of prime importance to the fellah are sugar, grown in the south, and rice and onions for export. Egypt scatters the last in their olfactory millions throughout Europe.

The handicraft of the fellah has changed less than his agriculture. The world is only interested in modifying his habits where change spells financial gain. Thus local crafts go on much as they have always done. Involving the traditional techniques of the artisan, they are today almost the only expression of a living aesthetic taste in Egypt. They are also another link with the civilization of the pharaohs, a civilization that probably produced more great craftsmen, and a more widely diffused sense of craft, than any other. These handicrafts of the villages are not to be confused with the brasswork, the ivory inlay, and the mother-of-pearl knick-knacks, which the bazaars turn out for the tourist. The fellah's products are primarily functional. The tiles that he bakes are not to be set on mantelpieces, and his baskets, of infinite pattern with their delicate variety of ornament, are for village use. The weavers' fine shawls, camel-hair blankets, and striped saddle-bags, are also for use not admiration. So, too, are the rugs in browns, buffs, and blues, woven by the women. Their usefulness and their simplicity are half their charm.

It is the same with the products of the potter, who remains the most talented and pleasing of the village craftsmen. Moulded by hand or turned on the wheel, his pots are one of the delights of Egypt. Unglazed, or decorated only with a plain red ochre pattern, they preserve simple traditional shapes. The delicate-throated water-coolers of porous clay that stand on window-sills, or the larger pots that the women carry on their heads from river and canal, are notes of formal grace, so frequently repeated that in time they pass unnoticed. As in pharaonic times, a rope is twisted round the larger pots just below their middle to preserve their shape during the process of sun-baking. This is removed when they enter the kiln. On Western pottery, which long since dispensed with this aid, the impression of a rope still often serves a purely decorative purpose. Thus we pay unconscious tribute to those who were among the earliest potters, and whose methods survive unaltered in the Nile valley.

Though a slave to his fields, under the dictation of his crops and of those who apportion his Nile water, the fellah is not always at labour. A restricted acreage, a swarming population, and limited industry, mean partial unemployment. Not everyone can work at once. In the East, where consciences are untroubled by a puritan or capitalist ethos, this is not always seen as a disaster. A pleasant vacancy is not repugnant to these people, and they have yet to suffer the white man's heaviest burden, the curse of boredom. There is always a dozing surplus, together with a mob of children, ready to rise and cluster round the stranger in any village. It is these happy unemployed who hour by hour play cards, draw out their draught-board on the ground, and in the shadow of a wall ponder their rudimentary chessmen. Though the Ptolemies tried to make athletics a feature of

Egyptian life, for the true native leisure is sedentary.

The fellah, working or idling, has an enviable un-quenchable gaiety and taste for entertainment. He finds the latter everywhere, and this makes his life tolerable. See him drinking coffee, smoking, teasing his friends, evoking laughter, or tapping his drum to the refrain of a song, and you realize that he has a genius for pleasure. Since hashish has been taken from him by white busy-bodies, this genius has discovered the gratifying effects that can be achieved with tea. (By brewing a stoup of tea again and again, he produces a thick black liquid with narcotic properties.) At the larger village markets, business forgotten, you will see him rapt, hanging on the lips of the professional story-teller, watching with delighted suspicion the adept conjurer, or learning his fortune once more from the wise man with second sight. He is at his best at festivals, such as the birthday of the Prophet or Shem-en-Nessim, 'the smelling of the Zephyrs'. The latter is in some ways the most picturesque festival in Egypt, for in April a whole people goes out to the fields to eat in the open air and greet the zephyrs of spring. It is then that they bring in decoratively plaited wheat, 'the bride of the corn', which is hung up in every house to bring good luck to crops and family for the coming year.

To see the fellah enjoying himself, or indeed the simple townsman, to appreciate the rich flavour of native Egypt, there is no better occasion than a large *mūlid* after dark in one of the provincial towns. You are swept along on a stream of laughing, shouting, pushing people. Cotton and silk are all around you; the mass flows, undulates and eddies. When the pressure eases, you find yourself with a multitude on a square before the brightly illuminated façade of a mosque. There are lights everywhere and they fall with

particular effect on the gay coloured awnings of the coffee-
houses and confectioners. Like the entrances to so many
hives, these hum and stir with sound and motion. Tall
poles with banners stretch far above the crowd and carry
the light into the night sky. A sherbet-seller in striped skirt
of red and white, carrying his iced refreshment slung from
his shoulder, clanks his metal cups like castanets. Sliced
water-melons, moist and glistening, show pink and green.
Stalls of sweetmeats are cascades of coloured crystal; beside
candied mango and children's fancies, sugar horses
copulate, the edible symbols of ancient fertility-rites. A
sherif, or would-be descendent of the Prophet, wears a faded
green turban; two or three Beduin, dark, sharp-featured,
altogether more Semitic, carry knives in their patterned
leather belts and blankets thrown over their shoulders; a
hollow-eyed withdrawn figure in severe dark coat and clean
white turban, wandering alone, is a student of Islam from
the University of al-Azhar; jostling negroid types bear
their tribal marks upon their cheeks; and inevitably
somewhere there is a blind beggar. Amid wild acclamation
passes a load of harlots, sitting cross-legged on a little flat
wagon. A contented white donkey draws them, indifferent
to the disturbance. As the priapic chariot passes and the
crowd thins, you notice family groups, islands so motionless
that you had missed them before. Sitting quietly on the
ground, eating a meal, even sleeping, they look as though
they had been encamped for days.

If you move into the narrow side-lanes the throng again
thickens; voice and gesture are inextricably mingled. It is
darker, though each booth diffuses an aura of light. Around
the chairs, outside each coffee-house, the crowd clots. It is
difficult to move. A story-teller, precise and informative, is
expounding one of his familiar tales. Beyond, with a hand

pressed against his cheek, a singer is jerking out the queer, torn, always seeming-nostalgic, songs of the Egyptians. They catch one in the pit of the stomach. To the sombre tapping of a hand upon a drum, two men, each with a staff, are rhythmically feinting and parrying, rhythmically advancing and retreating, manœuvring for the ideal vantage that is never won. Sculptural and statuesque, this dance, well executed, is one of the fine things of Egypt, and its fluent poses express in slow motion the essence of masculine grace and balance. The unhurried weaving of the staves, which seems nevertheless always to be approaching some climax, produces an accumulating effect of tension, and with the regular inescapable tap of the drum seems fateful.

Inside a discreet coffee-house there will be the *danse du ventre*. This from time immemorial has been performed by *ghazeeyahs*, gipsy dancing-girls, a race of unknown antiquity forming almost a distinct class. The maligned *danse du ventre* in its curiously detached and abstract quality is suited to Egypt and its landscape. Too often it is clumsily done, but that depends not on the dance but on the dancer. It can also be erotic, but usually to a Western eye the *ghazeeyahs* are fat and uninviting. The dance at its best evokes the essence of rhythm as one sees it in the uncurling snake or the pulsing sea-anemone. It is abstract and unromantic. The great *ghazeeyah* will employ a control of muscle and an economy of gesture comparable to that of the ballerina.

Amid the smoke and the lights, to the hilarious ribaldry of the audience and a subdued musical accompaniment, the dancing-girl takes the floor, probably naked to the waist. She is strung with a variety of gipsy ornaments and bangles; their sound when shaken emphasizes or counterpoints the main rhythms of the dance. Sometimes she uses castanets. The dance itself is a rhythmic swaying and undulation, produced by the perfectly controlled movement of every muscle in the dancer's torso. There may be embellishments and virtuosities, but such is the essence of the thing. So perfect is the control of these muscles, so absolute the *ghazeeyah's* training, that from her body she can evolve a first rhythm, from this modulate to a second, cross it with a third, while always maintaining a perfect sinuosity and concentration. One is reminded of things growing, of the natural world rather than the human. When the dance ends in a final quiver of intensity and the applause breaks out, one has the feeling of having witnessed something as impressive as the movement of the sea or the swirl of the Nile flood.

By now it will be late, but an insistent chant from somewhere down the street leads you on, and turning into a side-lane you find a strange spectacle. An old musician is touching a flute, and two rows of half-naked men, swaying and bowing in endless unison, chant the name of God. 'Al-lah, Al-lah, Al-lah.' Deprived of meaning and colour, the narcotic incantation is wrenched from hoarse dry throats. Sweat streams down their faces; the glazed eyes are without expression. These are 'barking' dervishes. For hours the ritual has continued unbroken; when a man falls exhausted, another takes his place. Drugged by this incantation, they are lost to themselves and their surroundings. There is great content in being lost to the fields and all they know.

This *zikr* or dervish dance is peculiarly the heart of the *mūlid*. It is the logical end of the fellah's festival gaiety which in a sense is an escape from living. Muhammad forbade wine, and the 20th century forbids hashish, so to this dark corner through the tumult of the streets some few have penetrated and will sway themselves into oblivion. 'Al-lah, Al-lah, Al-lah.' The incantation never falters; the Nile is silenced, the crops are gathered, and Egypt withers away. The fellah is with his desires.

———◆◆◆◆———

SIX

The Living and the Dead

Nowhere do you feel your mortality as in Egypt. Though the sun shines and the Nile offers its enchantments, you cannot escape 'the skull beneath the skin'. Despite the fecundity, the jostle of a close-packed population, death frames each vista, dominating the hurried gestures of the living. All down the Nile valley, the funerary temple, rock-hewn tomb, and staring pyramid are an unceasing *memento mori*. Admonishing, lifting the eye from the green cultivation to the desert edge, they intrude on privacy and temper the boldest enthusiasms.

The Egyptian has been acutely aware of the transitory nature of life from the earliest times. He lived on the soil and from the soil, and into the soil he would go. The facts were inescapable. Hence the Ancient Egyptians, perhaps more than any other people, found it necessary to gild the bitter pill and turned avidly to the possibilities of resurrection. A determined insistence on life after death reflected the undifferentiated state in which so many of them (one might recall the nameless multitudes who built the pyramids) passed their life on earth.

Thus arose mummification and the cult of resurrection, the flight from the damp alluvium of the Nile to the dry conserving desert. They early explored the possibilities of self-preservation, and bitumen has been found in the unambitious burials of 8000 B.C. With time a whole society, from the pharaoh downward, became organized for self-perpetuation in another world. Though pharaohs might build pyramids to make assurance doubly sure, there was mummification and a place on the desert edge to suit every purse. Even Kharga Oasis, 200 kilometres deep in the Libyan desert, contains a vast necropolis.

At all times death and the dead intruded upon the business of living. Recumbent along the desert edge, the 'Westerners'—for so they were called—imposed shamelessly upon the affairs of the valley. Throughout life men saved to buy a secure resting-place in death and accumulated obols for that final transit to the western bank of the Nile, whence they say arose the legend of the Styx. Even in revelry a future state was not permitted to be long out of mind, and a coffin carried round at feasts brought those present sharply back to earth. Death even invaded the sanctity of business, and a man at his wit's end might legally pledge his father's mummy.

The endless rock-tombs and pyramids, those ossuaries from which the stranger emerges blinking into the sunlight, are the best-known witness to the Egyptian concern with death. Bat-haunted, impervious to time, growing neither cooler in winter nor hotter in summer, they affirm and reaffirm, not that resurrection which they were meant to ensure, but the dominion of the grave. It is significant that so much known of Ancient Egypt should have been preserved in the papyri of the dead and their tombs. On thousands of walls, never meant for the eyes of the living, is depicted the life of a past civilization. The carved and painted figures in their perpetual dumb-crambo reveal all that time usually hides. There is the sowing and the reaping, the Nile's flood and fall, the labour of scribe and artisan, the hunting of the lion and the spearing of the fish; there is birth, marriage, war, festival and death. Upon the stone the slave creeps, the pharaoh stalks, and the stylized queen sits receiving fruits and homage. All this coming and going, the bustle and pomp of life, with the growth, florescence, and decay of a civilization, seem almost to have existed for the safety, honour, and delectation of the dead.

The number of carefully housed dead at Thebes, Abydos, and Memphis, is incomputable. Though robber and archaeologist shovel their way into the presence of the pharaohs, the vast majority of these sleepers are still safe under the sand. So many have died and been buried; and time in Egypt stretches far behind. One recalls Sir Thomas Browne: 'The number of the dead long exceedeth all that shall live. The night of time far surpasseth the day, and who knows when was the Aequinox?' In sand, in cliffs, under piles of stone, countless Ancient Egyptians were buried and preserved, at vast expense and with hope of resurrection.

None of these dead, we may reasonably presume, has risen. In this fact lies the pathos of the Nile valley; in this consists the *humanity* of the tombs and pyramids, compelling reverence from the stranger. He treads delicately in these places, confronted by the great delusions of men which paradoxically are more touching, and often nobler, than their manifold successes. His own frailty and fallibility, the tendency to error which no amount of reasoning can eliminate, the fundamental physiological limitation of man's mind, are apparent to him in these tombs. The wealth and energy that went to the building of these mausolea ran as inevitably to waste as they run in our own lives and times. Humanity has not altered in the short span of Egyptian history; only its delusions have changed. Remembering this, the stranger walks humbly through these great and futile monuments.

The ancient cult of the dead and the horror of corruption live most forcibly in the Valley of the Kings. When he had lain in state at the palace, stuffed with balsam, cassia and myrrh, each pharaoh of the New Kingdom, following fashion, came to this defile. Hewn out of the solid red rock, at a discreet distance from the babel of 'hundred-gated Thebes', the tomb-passages creep interminably into the darkness through chambers and antechambers. On the walls the mute figures posture and the hieroglyphs dribble out their tale of belief. Guarded by ponderous trapdoors of stone, in the recess of the last and farthest chamber, the mummy was left in its double, triple, casing, tricked out with gold and lapis. In the stuffy dry air, alone, the image of the dead king on the mummy case stared at the ceiling, waiting in vain the dispensation of Osiris and an end to mortal claustrophobia.

What an aristocracy this valley represented in its heyday! The most exclusive society in the world, for the pharaohs, at once both kings and gods, preserved their distance even in death. Here no lord or commoner by art or flattery could gain entrance; royalty was privileged to await alone a summons that never came. Even wives might not lie beside their kings. In the adjacent Valley of the Queens these kept in state their own rocky salons. Wrapped in gold-leaf and chastely coffined, they presented a galaxy of beauty and imperial grace unparalleled in courts above ground. But there were no movements and no voices. No opportunity came to unfold their jewelled charms in that eternal pleasance of gods and kings that they assiduously promised themselves. The resurrection of both kings and queens was altogether different, more sudden and brutal than they had anticipated. The robbers came. Trapdoors were forced, lanterns threw long shadows, hurrying feet and plebeian profanity echoed through the chambers. They were roughly shaken from their expectant immobility. The gold went, the jewels, and the alabaster vases. Wrappings were pulled from beauties as eagerly as if snatched by lovers. Mummy-cloths were stripped from kings like bandages from wounds. Pharaoh indeed was sold for balsam. Into this ruin, centuries later, came the curious; the early travellers, and then the archaeologists, gleaned what the robbers had left. Those who bought the shin-bone of a pharaoh for a few pence marvelled at its vulgar antiquity, but missed the ironical point—that such should be the end of persons who believed the next world as real as this and who had long and confidently laboured to enter it in a manner befitting their station.

Strangest of those who presumably awaited resurrection, but also found only robbers, were the sacred Bulls of Apis. The Serapeum at Sakkara, where these mummified beasts with their gold trappings lay far under ground, each in his vast granite sarcophagus, is one of the most interesting and surely one of the most sinister places in the world. Each bull in its lifetime was the representative of the god and in its death was buried here at infinite cost and with infinite labour. Around this strange personification there grew up in the Late Kingdom a powerful cult, and Alexander the Great himself came to pay homage to the god-beast. That such immense sarcophagi were manœuvred into place, and these huge creatures mummified and adorned as delicately as brides, is astonishing, yet perhaps less so than the weird misapplication of intelligence that the cult seems to represent. One has an impression of a terrifying moronic force at work, for the tombs reveal the endemic stupidity of man.

One grows aware that this stupidity is all about one, that it infects the saint as much as the sinner, and may find expression in one's own best-intentioned actions. These may have been good men who worshipped the bull, they were certainly good craftsmen and good engineers; but something obtuse in human nature turned their energy to madness and hollowed out a mausoleum for beef. The sense of a permanent and sinister kink in the human make-up is inescapable in the Tombs of the Bulls.

The consideration lavished on the Bulls of Apis was perhaps exceptional, but similar cults flourished throughout Egypt. From the centipede to the ibis the brute creation took on a symbolic meaning, and in the popular mind every field and farmyard became the home of animal deities. The Greeks claimed that in Egypt it was easier to find a god than a man, and Juvenal, not improperly shocked, asserted that 'whole towns worship a dog; but no one Diana.' At Bubastis the cult of the sacred cats was famous, and Latopolis, in Upper Egypt, owed its name to the *latus*, a large Nile fish, whose sacred mummies were still offered at a cheap rate to the 19th-century traveller. But it was perhaps at the vanished Crocodilopolis in the Fayum that the animal cult attained its most elaborate development. There, near the vanished labyrinth which Herodotus says was more impressive than the pyramids and a vaster undertaking than all the monuments of Greece, were kept the sacred crocodiles. These reptiles with bejewelled feet, the incarnation of a god, were forcibly fed by the faithful on cakes and honeyed drinks. Around those basking pampered monsters grew up a large and powerful priesthood with temples and ritual. The bland amphibians usurped the life and energy of a rich and prosperous district.

There was then, as there has always been in Egypt, an unusually wide gap between those who create ideas and those who use them. The essential substance of Egyptian religion differed greatly from its popular forms. Crocodiles were incidental to faith, and only the fellah saw gods in his fields. Among the instructed there was from early times belief in a supreme creator-god. The many 'gods' represented aspects of this deity and thus only in a limited fashion constituted a polytheism. It was natural that in the Egyptian climate the supreme god should most often have appeared in the character of the Sun, in which guise Ra daily slew the serpent of darkness and sailed across the heavens in his boat. With this fundamentally monotheistic framework were entwined, not only those cycles of older and newer deities which seem to overlap and oppose each other in every primitive mythology, but delightful mythic embroideries. Thus Seb, the god of the earth, and Nut, the goddess of the sky, were supposed to embrace at nightfall and only to be separated at morning by Shu, the god of light, who daily raised up the heavens.

But to understand the place of resurrection and religion in the Egyptian mind, it is necessary to grasp the myth, both moving and beautiful, that came to form an integral part, and indeed the most vital part, of Egyptian belief. Though the story of Isis and Osiris has many variants, its essential outline is always the same. Osiris, a man of divine origin, ruled in Egypt and, as the spirit of good, brought civilization and happiness to the country. After his murder by Set, the spirit of evil and desolation, his body cut in fourteen pieces was scattered throughout the lands. To recover her lord, Isis, his loving wife, set out on her sad wanderings. Having at last brought together his lost limbs at Philae, the 'lady of enchantments', as she was called, succeeded in reconstituting his body by magical formulae and bore a son by him. This son, Horus, in due course vanquished Set and established the supremacy of good over evil. It is as the mother of Horus that Isis became the 'divine mother', beloved of the Egyptians, who in innumerable statues is seen suckling her son. Finally Osiris, the divine man, with the help of Thoth, the god of wisdom, was restored to life and immortality, and took his place with the gods in the next world.

The importance of this legend as it relates to Egyptian ideas of resurrection cannot be exaggerated. Since Osiris had conquered death, there was no reason why others should not do so. There was hope for every mortal. 'As Osiris lives,' say the Pyramid texts, 'so shall he also live; as Osiris died not, so shall he also not die; as Osiris perished not, so shall he also not perish.' Osiris, by a natural extension of thought, from being simply a unique man resurrected, became not only a god himself but the cause and means of all resurrection. He was the advocate of mankind before the great gods: he interceded for them, remembering his own descent into death. The close parallels between Christianity and the Osiris story are clear. The god-man who suffers, dies, and is raised again, is familiar. As the Christian believes that, like Christ, he will be welcomed into the arms of the Father, so the Egyptian believed of his god-fearing neighbour that: 'The door of heaven is open unto thee, and the great bolts are drawn back for thee. Thou findest Ra standing there; he takes thee by the hand and leads thee into the holy place of heaven.' Isis and her divine conception of Horus are reflected in the story of the Virgin. Late statuettes of Isis seated with the infant Horus are often indistinguishable from the first Egyptian representations of the Virgin and the infant Jesus. It is not surprising that when Christianity reached Egypt it should have been widely received. The people found in the new religion the best features of the old, together with several not inconsiderable advantages.

Around the legend of Osiris there grew up a tremendous cult of resurrection, centred at Abydos, where his head was reputed to rest. The saviour even began to encroach on the prerogatives of Ra and the Osirid priesthood rivalled that of the great god. As the whole body of Osiris had been carefully preserved by Isis, so for thousands of years the dead Egyptians were mummified against their own resurrection. As Osiris had only won his immortality after successfully undergoing the scrutiny of the gods, so the dead mortal could only attain paradise after passing through the judgement hall of the immortals where his fate also hung in the balance. This conception of a judgement was the link between ethics and religion in Ancient Egypt. It was thus of extreme importance as a civilizing influence. Osiris, it was thought, would demand not only faith but works from the spirits who came to judgement.

But the safe passage past the heavenly tribunal, which every Egyptian hoped to make, was by no means assured to the good and the just. Success depended also upon ritual and formulae. When the mummy was left at last to the solitude of its tomb, it was not believed that the perishable body, wrappings and all, would stagger to its feet and consume the victuals left there. These were for the dead man's *Ka* or vital energy. The mortal body did not rise, and mummification merely provided a necessary *point de départ* whence the incorruptible and spiritual body might set out for the judgement hall of the gods. Arrived at the tribunal the spirit of the dead man insisted on his purity, and before a bench of forty-two gods his heart was weighed in the scales against the feather of righteousness and truth. Anubis, the jackal-headed, supported the balance, and Thoth inscribed on a papyrus the result of the test. If heart and feather balanced, the dead escaped the Devourer and passed on through the halls of the underworld. It was there that the abracadabra of the priests and the magical formulae upon the walls of his tomb were of vital importance. He had to run the gauntlet of immortal questioners and only his enchantments could provide him with the right answers, as once the enchantments of Thoth had provided safety for Osiris. This perilous transit accomplished, Thoth again awaited the dead man to introduce him into the presence of Osiris. It was at this moment that the endless inscriptions bearing the names of the dead served their purpose, for to reach the very threshold of the god without a name was the final peril in the ordeal after death.

Received by Osiris, who like himself died and rose again, the Egyptian's troubles were at an end. He was immortal and entered the confraternity of the gods. 'Thou shalt come forth unto heaven, thou shalt pass over the sky, thou shalt be joined unto the starry deities': such was the desire of the man on earth, and such he hoped his reward in heaven. Here ends the train of thought, the *élan* of desire, which from dynasty to dynasty carved tombs and raised temples, and which gave pharaonic civilization its special character.

The intrusion of the dead among the living persists in Islamic Egypt. In Cairo, a stone's throw from the light and warmth of the bazaars, lie the so-called Tombs of the Caliphs. No caliph reposes there (the earliest burial probably dates from Fatimid times), but this City of the Dead holds the famed memorials of the 15th-century Mamelukes. Once lavishly endowed, their domed tombs are associated with silent *madrasahs*, fountains now waterless, koranic schools without schoolboys, and empty chambers intended to receive the mourning families of those who built them. Many of these funerary complexes, with their beautifully patterned stone domes, such as those of Barkuk, Barsbay, and Kaytbay, are of immense architectural distinction. But they express—appropriately in such a setting—the last refined elegance that precedes decay. These tombs mark the end of the great tradition of Muslim architecture.*

From the streets thronged with the still-living, one passes abruptly to the adjacent dead. The categories of right and wrong, the reflexes of hate and desire, are suddenly confronted with the silencing silence of tombs. By starlight or under the subtle showmanship of the moon one walks through a city that holds only bones. No sound but the echo of a footfall, and only the night watchmen witness one's passage. Under exquisite domes, outlined black against the sky, mortuary palaces in their magnificence, lie rulers long since dead, while in smaller mausolea the remains of 19th-century pashas are still completing their methodical decomposition. One's feet stir the dust and one strives painfully to distinguish between oneself and the dwellers in this city. But the silent streets offer no consolation; the tombs are as real as were the lighted thoroughfares, and this sleeping congregation is as real as the moving crowds. As one wanders on, little seems to differentiate the living from the dead; both are part of one comprehensive process whose unity the Nile valley emphasizes. One is closer to bones than one had been led to believe by rubber-tyred hearses and the funerary deceptions of the West.

Even in the villages of the cultivation, cemeteries elbow the living and tombs insinuate themselves persistently between the houses. Sometimes the cemetery is the village

* See Chapter 9 for *madrasahs* and Mameluke architecture.

square. But more often the Muslim cemeteries lie on the desert edge. As the Ancient Egyptians visited the tombs of their ancestors, so the fellahin pay the weekly ceremony of Et-Tala' or the 'going up'. To silent, wind-swept, and usually dilapidated graves, made of mud-brick and sometimes whitewashed, the women from the villages and a sprinkling of men 'go up' on the day when the dead are said to return and for a few hours inhabit their sepulchres. The procession that straggles out from the village will comprise one or more devout men engaged to recite passages from the Koran—recitations are supposed to be particularly beneficial to the dead—and often professional mourners like those of Ancient Egypt. The women take with them special ring-shaped loaves as a wage both for the holy men and the wailers. Groups of well-defined black-robed figures huddle beside the tombs in the buff, indeterminate desert. The wind licks up little funnels of sand that in the sunlight go skidding over the ground. A wife bent over her husband's tomb cries, in an almost matter-of-fact voice: 'Good day, O Hasan! How are you?' Such familiar greeting, such one-sided conversations, break the silence along the desert edge.

Though the dead now look towards Mecca and not to the setting sun, the end of life is hardly less ritualistic than it was in the past. To loose the soul with certainty from the alluvial anonymity of the valley and the village, the fellahin of Upper Egypt until recently sacrificed a ram or kid and its blood was sprinkled upon the spot where death occurred. A body, borne on a bier and wrapped in green, the colour sacred to the prophet, is still carried to a graveyard in the safety of the desert, whenever such is accessible. It is followed by mourners with dust upon their heads, and to a frantic complaining moves out of the orbit of the Nile and draws purposefully away from the soil, the water, and the agricultural round, which dominated it for a lifetime.

In the final analysis something more than pharaonic tombs and Muslim cemeteries seems to make death ever present in this valley. It is the distance that separates the stranger from the anonymous multitude of the fellahin. Having little contact with the dark-eyed, bare-footed, cotton-clad figures in the fields, the stranger does not see individuals and personalities but units: so many human units living in a certain way and situated at varying points on a line between birth and death. Beauty, character, eminence, anything which differentiates a man from his fellows, obscures in some degree the lot which he shares in common with them all. Death is axiomatic for the masses, but there is never the same absolute certainty that it applies to the exceptional individual. There is no exact parallel to invoke. So kings have grown to believe themselves immortal. For the stranger, isolated from the toiling Nile dwellers, there are no individuals and death appears over every face. There is a story that Alexander the Great, seeking to establish his divine origin, visited the oracle of Jupiter-Ammon at Siwa Oasis, where a particle of dust lodged in his eye. A temple priest thought fit to remind the conqueror that 'of this dust are made the kings of Macedon'. Alexander would have needed no such reminder, if he had sensed the temper of Egypt.

SEVEN

Things made with Hands

Rock-tomb, pyramid, and temple succeed in the endlessly similar, endlessly changing landscape. In a sense inapplicable to Classical and Gothic ruins, these buildings are desolate. It is not simply that purpose left most of them before the Huns sacked Rome, but that for so many centuries they were then removed from the lives and emotions of men. No one living understood their significance or the civilization which built them. Even today, measured, restored, visited, they are difficult to comprehend. How should the 20th century know the heart of Sekhmet the lion-goddess, or fear, like Herodotus, even to pen the name of Osiris? Though portrayed in numberless bas-reliefs, the gods are irrevocably gone. Dragomen may point to the divine symbols on the walls, but Ra is of no account in his own palaces. Time has stolen the life of the building. Here indeed is the 'vieille usine désaffectée de dieu'. There are no votaries in the court of the temple, no ritual, no priests in the sanctuary: only the daily shaft of sun dropping between the pillars, burning the cracked and prostrate god; only the appraising abstracted scrutiny of Baedeker. The descendants of the fellahin who laboured to erect the buildings (and under archaeological masters often labour to erect them once again) ignore the wanderings of Isis and the name of Set. Here the gods have died sooner than the works of men.

The setting of the ruins that still dominate the valley is incomparable. Egypt is made for ruins. In this dry climate, no clumps of nettle or bramble sheathe the lapsed wall, no rains deface the carving on the stone. Pillar and cornice fall and there they safely lie, unless buried by the drift of conserving sand. Palms wave alongside temple walls, green bee-eaters sit swaying on their fronds, doves circle the empty courts, and, sparkling in the sun, is the river with white sails and echoing voices. The river is an essential adjunct to the temples. Perhaps alone it still understands them. From Aswan, whence came by water the granite for colossus and obelisk, to Memphis, where a little sphinx in the days of basin irrigation used to wet its paws in the flood, the Nile provides the magnificent setting for the Egyptian past.

If this setting is exceptional, so is the pervading sense of time and history. The temples and the stories on their walls, the pyramids and the furniture of the tombs, have more to tell and are more fascinatingly informative about the past than other ancient remains. They are first-hand history: a curious, startling ledger of lost events and thoughts. The stranger is privileged to look, as it were through the eyes of the Sphinx, at the first considerable human society; he traces in detail its rapid development; he watches its slow decay. Egyptian art presents, more graphically than that of any other country, a summary of human activity over a long and remote period. It portrays indifferently the state of gods and pharaohs or the comings and goings of obscure individuals. With meticulous faithlessness the little figures on the walls betray the secrets of changing generations, remorselessly exposing the fancies, habits, and beliefs of thirty dynasties. Cheops built his tomb in the bowels of the Great Pyramid in the faith that Osiris would raise him from the dead; in the reign of Justinian people were still mummified at Philae in the same belief. At the Step Pyramid of Sakkara rises the earliest monumental building in the world; at Tell el-Amarna is preserved something of the civilization created by Akenaton, 'the first individualist in history'; at Thebes may be deciphered the exploits of the most ancient military empire. In time and in scope the canvas is immense. Even Europe becomes involved in this Nile pageant. The forms of Greek art are foreshadowed in the rock-tombs of Beni-Hassan; the Parthenon, it seems, may owe something to Karnak; Juvenal was an exile at Aswan; and fifteen Roman emperors left their cartouches on the walls of Esna. The hypostyle hall at Dendera was finished while Christ was in Jerusalem; the temple of Luxor housed a Copto-Byzantine church; and a band of Christian monks practised asceticism on the site of the Memphian necropolis. From Menes, first king of the 1st Dynasty, to the Graeco-Roman tourists who wrote their names on the Colossi of Memnon, history files by.

The pyramids of Giza have come to epitomize the long Egyptian past, but a first impression of these stone mountains is disappointing. They are less breathlessly imposing than might be expected: no geometrical shape conceals volume as effectively as a pyramid and there is nothing to measure them against except a blue sky. Though the Great Pyramid of Cheops, built of over 2 million limestone blocks, is a mountain 450 feet high covering thirteen acres, statistics seem to mean little. One can merely agree with Dr. Johnson that pyramids are 'the most bulky works of manual industry'. It is only when one has lived with the pyramids and felt them overshadowing the valley that they attain their stature. By day they watch one's ridiculous actions, at night their dark wall obscures the stars, and far out in the desert they stand up, gigantic signposts, pointing the way to Egypt. A sense of their scale and durability sinks in. Man's most indestructible creations, they will probably see him off the earth. For 2,000 years rumour and speculation surrounded these impassive tombs. They were thought to hold 'the ghosts of Ptolemies' lewd race,' or even to be the granaries of Joseph, and Herodotus in his rarest vein reported that Cheops built the Great Pyramid with the help of a loose daughter's ill-gotten gains. Given the size and cost of the pyramid, her achievement might seem almost as remarkable as the monument itself. Imagination still works upon them, for though we know their fruitless office, we choose to find in them signs and symbols.

A spice of danger attends the climbing of Kephren's pyramid. It is three feet lower than the Great Pyramid, but with base lines that are shorter (690 as opposed to 755 feet), the angle is over 50 degrees, and the apex retains some 110 feet of the smooth ashlar casing that originally clad both pyramids. They must then have been white and shining presences. The ascent is best made in the early morning, when the mist, still heavy on the Nile valley, obscures their bulk, when camels loom suddenly on the road and fellahin pass like ghosts on their way to the fields. At the base of Kephren, the Beduin guide is waiting. It is cold as you prepare for the ascent, and only the lowest courses of the pyramid are visible. You climb. The blocks are friable and need a wary eye. Each calls for a long step up. The guide has tucked his *galabiyeh* round his waist and always just ahead are his brown legs and carbuncled leathery feet. Below and above, all is lost in mist; the crumbling ledges as you mount are silent. Then unexpectedly you come to a region of habitation. There are chicken bones, rats' skins, the castings of an owl, and a falcon's feathers. The deserted rock has been the scene of animal feasts and traffic; they mate here and doze in the sun. A jackal disappears along a ledge, a raven slips into the mist, croaks, and is lost.

Then comes a sudden sense of sunlight and blue sky above. Emerging from its collar of cotton-wool, there is a glimpse of the rosy apex of Kephren. You have reached the limestone casing. There is a small overhang and difficulties are about to begin. Your guide offers a brief prayer to Allah, and you no doubt recall the warning in the *Guide Bleu*: 'L'ascension de cette pyramide exige de grands efforts ... la partie revêtue ... est dépourvue d'asperités et ne donne aucune prise à l'escalade.' In fact the casing has conveniently weathered in four and a half millennia; notches and fissures offer hand and foothold. You edge your way up from mist into the sun. It falls hot on your back and the casing proves longer than you expected. Then suddenly there is nothing above, and you stand on a few square feet of broken summit. From a crevice the guide pulls out a metal case and extracts a book. It is (wrongly) dedicated 'To Mark Twain, the first foreigner to climb the Second Pyramid.' You sign. There is a feeling of achievement. Lying in the sun and silence of the early morning you are detached from the lower world. Exhilarated by the climb, by the last smooth courses of the pyramid, you seem to have a claim on its past.

The mist burns off the valley. The stone casing slopes steeply away and Egypt beneath harnesses itself to another day's work. A voice floats up from the desert and, in the green fields beyond, you note the movement of pygmies. Cars edge down the road from Cairo and tourists are mounting their bored camels in front of the Mena House Hotel. Behind, stretches the desert in the complexity of fold and undulation; in front lies Cairo with its 7 million; to the north is the Delta, and trending endlessly southward is the bright green Nile valley between its hills. In a single sweep you take in a whole country, and like a confident showman present to the imagination one detail after another. Throned on the past, you cavalierly eye the present, and for an hour or so belong to no century. When you make a careful descent, there is the impression of dropping into an unfamiliar world. It takes time to realize that you live and have a temporary being on the level and in the present.

Wherever antiquity, presented in carved and mellowing stone, lies in ruins southward from Cairo, the Egyptian past is arresting. But are these ruins beautiful? What formal qualities characterize Egyptian architecture? How do the temples compare with those of Greece, or with the churches of Byzantium, the villas of Palladio? How does the statuary look beside the charioteer from Delphi, the saints of Chartres, or the work of Brancusi? Divested of their romantic and historic interest, what is the aesthetic importance of these antiquities?

The character of the Ancient Egyptian suggests an answer. A notably good husband and father, he lived in a well-planned sensible house. Taking ever-renewed pleasure in the Nile landscape, he was, even when a city-dweller, an observant countryman. Normally cheerful, industrious and disciplined, he was above all practical. He pursued his science, his medicine, his learning, for good matter-of-fact reasons. As a believer, he was more concerned with ritual than with dogma, and there was nothing transcendental about his view of the next world which he envisaged as a more agreeable extension of the present. Member of a balanced and confident society, he was as little subject to personal neuroses as to external pressures. Consequently he saw little reason for inquiry or change. The old methods and ideas served well and he clung to them. What had been was sufficient. Even in the Old Kingdom education consisted mainly in copying. The textbooks have survived and show each generation contentedly and meticulously reproducing the knowledge their fathers had acquired. Unattracted by abstract speculation, the Egyptian rarely valued thought for its own sake. He was the least visionary of men.

From such characteristics much follows. The Egyptian's feeling not only for nature but for the simple satisfactory activities of daily life found vigorous expression in his art. He never ceased to be delighted with all he saw. Even when beliefs and ideas became immutably fixed, the eye remained observant. This accounts for much of the charm of his wall-paintings and bas-reliefs. Using a diagrammatic shorthand (not unlike that of many 20th-century painters), he told his story with unfailing success. In the Tombs of the Nobles, where art remained in closer contact with life than in royal tombs and temples, representations of birds and animals, of the processes of agriculture, of business and pleasure, show extraordinary vitality, for they were based on visual impressions and not on conceptions.

Again, practical people are usually good with their hands. The Egyptians were craftsmen *par excellence*. From craftsmanship derived a sense of materials. They seem to have known instinctively the best medium—hard or soft stone, diorite, alabaster, wood or metal—for the particular work in hand. From craftsmanship derived also sophistication, careful detailing, and unusual delicacy of touch. These are among the qualities which make Tutankhamun's tomb furniture so attractive. Not surprisingly, these observant craftsmen invented portraiture. Though usually made to be immured in tombs, the portraits that have come down to us, particularly the lay figures such as the famous Sheikh el-Beled, are clearly faithful and penetrating representations.

Not until the Romans developed the portrait bust were such likenesses repeated.

Other elements in the Egyptian character had a less happy influence on art and architecture. In the long run traditionalism and preoccupation with symbol and ritual proved disastrous. Pre-dynastic art opens with a series of beautiful objects, metal implements, diorite jars, and so on. At Sakkara, in the 3rd millennium B.C., this original aesthetic sensibility is unimpaired. But soon the effects of a lack of intellectual excitement and curiosity are apparent. Forms grow stereotyped and lose their vitality. There is little sense of growth or discovery. Art, like education, law, and medicine, ceased to develop. Insensitive to new influences, it fell back upon craftsmanship. One is aware of extreme technical sophistication linked to intellectual and emotional immobility. The Egyptian possessed the sensitive hand and the practical competence to produce anything, but sometimes for centuries the creative image failed to suggest itself. So intense did conservatism become that it eventually found expression in nostalgia. Art carefully retraced the few steps it had taken since the days of the Old Kingdom. Only the expert can distinguish many of the works of the 26th Dynasty from those produced 2,000 years earlier. Undue attachment to symbol and ritual played a disastrous role. For lack of some creative stimulus, a perfervid symbolism led not to that imaginative shorthand which symbols aim to create but to constriction and abstract complexity. Once art had ceased to move, the established modes of sculpture, painting, and architecture became associated with vested interests. It was not only difficult but politically dangerous to modify accepted canons. Royal and priestly control so constrained and ritualized the art of the Nile that for long periods it ceased to be a vital form of expression.

It was of course precisely in this aesthetic coma that the sense of craftsmanship was invaluable. Though Egypt for centuries produced little great art, she produced little that was downright bad.

Strangely enough it is those famous and ambitious works, the cult and funerary temples of Upper Egypt, that most clearly indicate, in terms of architecture, where the antiquities of Egypt may fail to satisfy. The temple pattern that developed there in the 2nd millennium B.C. with the almost limitless imperial resources of the New Kingdom remained virtually unaltered until the temples were closed by the Emperor Theodosius in the 4th century. These temples were designed to impress by sheer size. The exploitation of mass can of course be significant, and in front of the Great Pyramid at Giza it is relevant to recall Gaudier-Brzeska's dictum' 'Sculpture is the mountain.' But the temples of Upper Egypt are sometimes merely ponderous. Even the axial planning, the progression through forecourt and hypostyle to a narrow sanctuary, is more effective ritually than architecturally. Buildings of architectonic inspiration—the courtyard of Amenophis III at Luxor, the second courtyard at Medinet Habu, or the temple of Hatshepsut—stand out by exception. The architectural sensibility they express is generally foreign to the Nile, and the temples of Ancient Egypt repeatedly fail to achieve the harmony and balance which are the essence of great building. The failing is primarily one of intellectual vitality, of the power to combine disparate parts into a single harmonious whole. In the stylized wall-carvings of the temples are found the native genius for line, detail, and execution; in the temples themselves one may often seek in vain the formal relationships and creative tensions that arise from avid inquiry.

A Greek temple is co-ordinated; each part bears a relationship of balance to every other. The building is also proportioned to the human figure. The scale of the celebrants relates to the architecture; they do not creep, as must have done the priests of Ammon-Ra, like mites, round the base of towering masonries. It is significant that the Egyptians in their temples never explored the possibilities of enclosed space. Their weighty hypostyles remained crowded halls of passage. Nowhere is insensibility to architectural form more apparent than in the famous hypostyle at Karnak. This gigantic chamber is said to be large enough to contain Notre-Dame, yet here is weight without mass, and size without splendour. The vast swollen pillars are flabby and spineless, and their proximity destroys any sense of height or perspective. It remains a monument to all that determination, labour and craftsmanship can fail to achieve. The gods at Karnak were more grandiloquently, but less adequately, served than they had been in Zoser's mortuary temple at Sakkara over 1,500 years earlier.

Superbly set, immense, invested with extraordinary historic interest, the antiquities of the Nile are always imposing, and often initially overwhelming. Doubts arise later. Something is lacking in these monumental and repetitive temples and tombs. It is something found in the simple alabaster and diorite jars of the pre-dynastic period, in the restraint of Imhotep's buildings at Sakkara, in the statuary of the 12th Dynasty, in the reliefs of the sanctuary of Seti I at Abydos and in those of the tomb of Ramose at Thebes. It is found, perhaps above all, in every work from Tell el-Amarna, where the genius of Akenaton, breaking the bonds of tradition, profoundly disturbed and stimulated his countrymen. This something is a sense of form.

———◆◆◆◆◆———

EIGHT

The City of Alexander

Menelaus returning from Troy was becalmed off the future
site of Alexandria on the island of Pharos, and got safely
under sail, so Homer relates, only by outwitting the sea-god
Proteus. It was the existence of this off-shore island, with
its safe anchorage, that prompted Alexander the Great in
331 B.C. to found his new city on the low limestone ridge
that lay between the island and the inland lake of Mareotis.
On his death in 323, Ptolemy Soter, his chief-of-staff and
ablest of his Macedonian generals, seized Egypt and
established his capital at Alexandria. He also took the wise
precaution of seizing his master's body which he buried
there in imperial state.

The rule of the Ptolemies, before it ended with the
troubled glory of Cleopatra, lasted almost 300 years. It was
essentially Greek rule; Cleopatra, last of her line, alone
bothered to learn the Egyptian tongue. As E. M. Forster
put it: 'Up in Egypt [the Ptolemies] played the Pharaoh,
and built solemn archaistic temples like Edfu and Kom
Ombo. Down in Alexandria they were Hellenistic.' It was a
Mediterranean, not an Egyptian, capital.

Effective and imaginative, the rule of the first three
Ptolemies—Soter, Philadelphus, and Euergetes—spanned
more than a century, and they made Alexandria the greatest
city of its time. On the island rose the fort and towering

lighthouse of the Pharos, one of the seven wonders of the
ancient world. Built by Sostratus, the 3rd-century contemporary of Euclid and Eratosthenes, it was over 400 feet
high and its great mirror cast a beam thirty-five miles. At
the same time the island was linked to the mainland by a
mole, the Heptastadion (= seven stades, i.e. over three-
quarters of a mile long), thus creating twin harbours: the
harbour of Safe Return to the west, and the Great or Royal
Harbour to the east. The harbours, which could berth, it was
said, 1,200 ships did not silt up as the off-shore current
carried the sediment brought down by the Canopic Nile
firmly eastward. The port was also linked by canal to Lake
Mareotis, and so to the Nile. Sea-trade bore outward from
the Pharos the special products of Egypt: glass, papyrus,
perfumes (a state monopoly), and immense quantities
of grain. From the Lebanon, vessels put in with purple dye
and timber, always a scarcity in the Nile valley, and from
further afield came honey, olive oil, and marble for the
buildings of the city.

The latter was laid out symmetrically on a grid plan, each
district denoted by a letter of the Greek alphabet, and the
Canopic Way, 100 feet wide and three miles long, traversed
it from west to east. By the 1st century B.C. there were
some 300,000 Greek citizens, and perhaps a total population
of half a million including a large Jewish community. On the
Great Harbour was situated the royal quarter, a town in
itself, and to the south of the harbour lay both the
Mouseion, the university where generations of brilliant
scholars and scientists found free board and lodging, and
the Library with perhaps half a million payprus rolls (of
which Callimachus was at one time custodian). Yet farther
south rose the Serapeum, the famous temple where
Serapis, the city's tutelary deity (the astute invention of

Ptolemy Soter and his religious advisers), was worshipped with his Egyptian consort Isis. Set on the edge of blue water, it was a brilliant city in the literal sense, for many of the stone buildings were stuccoed with a gypsum of dazzling whiteness. Alexandria shone.

It was no less brilliant intellectually. Here Callimachus wrote the poem on the death of his friend Heraclitus which echoes down the centuries; here Theocritus came to live and described in his 15th Idyll a typical Alexandrian family outing on the Feast of Adonis. But it was in the fields of mathematics, geometry, astrology, medicine and philology that the Ptolemaic city excelled. Euclid propounded the elements of geometry; the astonishing polymath Eratosthenes calculated the diameter of the globe (correct to within fifty miles); Herophilus anticipated Harvey's discovery of the circulation of the blood; a scientist postulated that the earth went round the sun seventeen centuries before Copernicus; another devised the first accurate calendar, making provision for leap years; and the scholarly methods of the Mouseion gave birth to the first textual criticism. The mixture of science, wit, imagination, and royal patronage that characterized the city in the 3rd century is vividly evoked by the story of Berenice's hair. When, in 244, the much-praised wife of Ptolemy Euergetes hung up her locks in the temple of Aphrodite at Canopus, as an ex-voto for the safe return of her husband from campaign, they were stolen (Ptolemaic society was not remarkable for its honesty). But Conon, the astronomer, providentially discovered a new constellation at that moment, and the Queen's hair was translated to the heavens to shine as the group of stars we have known ever since as Coma Berenice. Callimachus duly celebrated the event in verse.

But the great Ptolemies passed, and lesser kings succeeded.

The dynasty struggled dimly on, until with Cleopatra, wedded successively to the 14th and 15th Ptolemies, it flared in 30 B.C. to its dramatic end. Rome, whose covetous eye had rested on Alexandria for over a century, was the beneficiary. Octavian, coldly efficient, turned the province of Egypt into an imperial granary and the harvests of the Nile provided bread for the circuses of Rome. Though the Alexandrians in the Byzantine period were to play a crucial role in the development of Christianity, the exciting days were over.

When Alexandria in 640 fell to the Arabs, decline continued. The collapse of the lantern of the Pharos, surmounted by the statue of Poseidon, in about 700 was symbolic. Arab civilization which brought such splendour to Cairo was fatal to a city which has always drawn its inspiration and vitality from the Mediterranean. While Christians squabbled, and Muslims ruled without regard to seaborne trade, Alexandria atrophied. The Arab walls of the 9th century enclosed only a fragment of the Ptolemaic city. Sediment in the 12th century closed the Canopic branch of the Nile, and as silt accumulated against the Heptastadion an isthmus developed between the Pharos and the mainland. A 17th-century Englishman found Alexandria's 'beauties perished' and 'nothing left her but ruins', while Lord Sandwich's party in 1738 recorded that it was 'almost destitute of inhabitants'. When Muhammad 'Ali Pasha, an Albanian and the semi-independent representative of the Porte in Egypt, turned his shrewd attention to the place in 1815, the metropolis had dwindled to a few thousand. By linking it to the Nile with a new canal, by introducing cotton-crops, and above all by welcoming back Greeks and Levantines, the pasha made Alexandria once again a great commercial centre.

Rich and sophisticated, this second Alexandria had

become, in the first half of the 20th century, an agreeable if not a noble city. A corniche stretched for thirteen miles past a series of delightful beaches. It was terminated at either end by a royal palace; that at Montaza was distinguished for its vulgarity. Unfortunately the town was also a notable example of ribbon development. Behind the corniche, and separating it from desert and cultivation, stretched a belt of housing. This strip of habitation offered surprising contrasts: at one point, a mile or more deep, it comprised hotels, a race-track, and a golf-course; at another the open fields were barely a stone's throw from the sea; one-room tenements nudged palatial villas, and bathing-boxes and a native laundry were wedged between a cabaret and a casino. King Cotton who built it had no eye for planning.

Yet in summer, when a cooling breeze blew steadily from the sea and the sun shone, the visitor was ready to forget this architectural hotchpotch and the standards which it seemed to symbolize. In this affluent Graeco-Levantine society, pleasure was almost as easily come by as in the days of the Ptolemies. The sea-air was conducive to love and gossip; there was splendid bathing and the best cooking in Egypt. At this season, the place seemed in perpetual fête. Yet there was an unreality about the festivities. They were not to last.

Today the second Alexandria has disappeared almost as decisively as the city of the Ptolemies. The bankers and the cotton barons have fled to Switzerland, the scholars and poets are dispersed, and with the cast of The Alexandria Quartet the nymphs and satyrs have departed. Villas are shuttered or expropriated, gardens are overgrown, and the dubious cafés evoked in the poems of Cavafy are unrecognizable. The Greeks have again left Alexandria. These changes are understandable. Until 1960 this was hardly an Egyptian city. Turning its back firmly on the Delta, as did the Ptolemaic capital, it looked seaward. It was clever, spirited, ecumenical. Such a place, where half the street signs were in Roman script and not in Arabic, was unacceptable to a nationalist Egypt. Alexandria had to change. The disappearance of the international city was inevitable, perhaps even justifiable, but it was sad.

Its successor is something of a ghost. Alexander, Cleopatra, Hadrian and his friend Antinous, loom larger in the imagination than the people on its melancholy streets. So strong is this sense of the past that, on a bright summer morning, it almost seems as though the inadequate reality might disappear. One would wake to find Macedonians pouring out of the catacombs, and the Canopic Nile in full flood between those dotted lines that preserve its memory on large-scale maps. Ptolemy Philadelphus with his poets would lead again that procession which once was the gaze of the city. There would be the Sileni clad in purple and vermilion cloaks, crowned with ivy wreaths of beaten gold and green enamel, bearing the caduceus and gilded lamps of ivy-wood. Youths in golden crowns would follow, and women carrying lilies, aspergers of scent, and golden dishes of cinnamon, amaracus, spikenard, and essence of fenugreek. Down the corniche borne on palanquins with silver feet, under embroidered canopies, would appear the beauty of the time with garlands of peach-blossom and branches of palm; and the priests of Dionysus would pour libations, and athletes bear their Delphian tripods before the emblematic figures of Night and Day, of Earth and Heaven. And last, behind the oryxes and Ethiopian birds, behind the white hornless cattle and the panthers, behind the chariot of Bacchus and the winepress, where sixty satyrs trampled out the grapes singing to the music of silver flutes, would appear once more the statue-image of Alexander, crowned with a chaplet of ivy leaves, coming to take possession of his city.

Little enough remains of that city. The mud that silted the mouths of the Nile dimmed its brightness; channels of thought were choked; sects wrangled where philosophers had discussed. A few blocks of granite recall the Pharos; the royal palace and the Mouseion are gone without trace; the Christians burnt the Library; ladies of the khedivial family are entombed on the spot where Alexander is said to have been buried; scholars dispute the exact site of Canopus, the fashionable Ptolemaic watering-place; and the obelisks which once graced the temples of Artemis and Arsinoe were long since shipped to Rome and Constantinople. The grace and style, the delights and speculations, which came to the Delta with the Greeks were easily lost. It was not possible to mummify the speed of intellect, the zest for life, which made Ancient Alexandria hum. A few Romans tried to keep up the tradition, but they lacked the touch. The mind of Ptolemaic Alexandria alone survives: the history of Manetho, the spidery lines of Euclid, Eratosthenes's computations, an idyll by Theocritus, a poem by Callimachus, and the epigrams of Alexandrian wits. One remembers 'nailed upon the night Berenice's burning hair', and Philadelphus sacrificing his reputation to obtain the manuscripts of Sophocles.

Yet the Hellenes even today have their rallying points. The sea remains. Alexandria lives on its beaches, and the first attraction of the place is also its most intimate link with the past. Along the corniche a wave curls in a dozen sunlit bays, catches the light, spills and runs nimbly up the sand. Farther out white spray shoots over the reefs and falls into the safety of quiet blue water. When the Greeks first came they brought something of the lucent quality of the Aegean. This quality, a curious infusion of light in water, makes one always turn one's head in Alexandria towards the sea. As it holds Nelson's ships and the weed-covered blocks of stone that were once the Pharos, so one imagines the sea to hold in solution the whole past of the city. Deeply blue in calm summer and rustling at the edge of many bays, it seems tense with association, as though it could barely carry its heavy historical precipitate. In such a stillness Menelaus returning from Troy beached at the island of the Pharos, and Pompey the Great, as he was rowed towards the Pelusiac shore, sensing his treacherous end, bowed his head deeper over the dialogue of Plato. On such a glazed sea, where the fishing-boats today slide almost windless into harbour, Cleopatra's barge put out to the stroke of silver oars that dipped to the music of a flute. Alexandrian waters that hissed under her prow still preserve the memory of such occasions.

There is also in the town, recently excavated, a late Hellenistic theatre and street. The ruins are favoured by hoopoes. Running parallel to the old Canopic Way, the street, probably buried for 1,000 years, is remarkably preserved. The shop-fronts, the entrance to the ample baths, and the very street paving, survive. Down this street Cleopatra will have passed borne on her litter. Her sandals may even have touched these stone slabs. Beyond, if you take your way through a dusty slum, you will find yourself again in the ghostly past of the city. From a jumble of inexplicit ruins rises Pompey's grandiloquent pillar. Its 100 feet of polished granite sail through the sky. Stunted green trees grow haphazard round its base, and flights of pigeon circle about it. Though tenements are only a stone's throw away, the site is immersed in a curious silence. Voices and the sound of traffic reach you as through the cloak of time. This pillar, all that survives of a vast and magnificent complex, is oddly inviolate. To the north stood the Mouseion, the greatest seat of learning in the ancient world; adjacent was the imposing temple of Serapis. The pillar itself, which was not raised by Pompey the Great but by an obscure and flattering citizen to the honour of Diocletian, was the centre of a colonnade of 400 columns. Near by were housed the 200,000 volumes which Antony seized from Pergamum and presented to Cleopatra, and which no doubt included the poems of Nicander and Musaeus, the Homeric text edited by Crates of Mallos, and the history of Apollodorus the Athenian. This gigantic theft ended the intense collectors' rivalry between Pergamum and Alexandria, a rivalry that prompted the Ptolemies to forbid the export of papyrus, hoping that a lack of raw material might stop the production of Pergamese manuscripts. It is easy to envisage the wild excitement of the savants and students of the Mouseion when this unrivalled cargo reached the city. Under their itching fingers lay half the wisdom that history, so far as they knew, had spared.

The enchanting figurines in the Graeco-Roman Museum, perhaps the most important relics of the art of Ptolemaic Alexandria, must have appealed to a very different set of people. These terracottas, the best dating from the time of Alexander, recall the famous collection found at Tanagra, but the climate of Egypt has been kinder than that of Greece and they have preserved their delicate colouring. In these graceful miniature people we see the very crowd that thronged the streets to watch Philadelphus's procession. Fancy can be left on the seashore, for here are the informal portraits of the ghosts that imagination chases past tenements and through the asphalt streets. From the showcases the quick, gay, and frivolous Ptolemaic city looks out. Here are not the scholars of the Mouseion, but the entertaining wives of the rich, courtesans, roués, dandies, poets, and the tough operators of the maritime market. These figures have an immortal chic. The women's hair is set in the height of fashion and the men have a knowing air. A wag is laughing at his own joke, and a smiling lady beside him lifts her skirt to show an admirable leg. They skate on thin ice and the art of the sculptor is such that it never breaks. The figures, like the civilization they represent, are gracefully intelligent, light and sophisticated. Were these people ever dowdy or solemn? Did they ever come down to earth, run out of amaracus and lilies, spill wine on those delightful dresses, or wake to a gloomy day? One realizes before these showcases that such a society was too precious to last, too witty and aerated to keep going in the dull persistence of time. Grace and decadence went hand in hand. How could these entertaining and civilized people have dealt with the encroaching Nile silt, Islamic intensity, or the extreme demands of Christ? They were too clever for the Middle Ages.

But not all this Hellenized society was killing time with grace and volatile intelligence. Westward from Alexandria stretched for fifty miles the freshwater lake of Mareotis.

Fed from the Nile, and separated from the sea by an isthmus two or three miles broad, this stretch of water was the focus of a number of quiet semi-Greek communities leading a simple agricultural life. Existence on the shores of this inland sea must have approached the idyllic, and the sober gait of events provided a reassuring contrast to the pace and glitter of the capital. It was at Plinthine on the north shore that grapes, according to legend, had first been made into wine, and in Ptolemaic times carefully tended vineyards stretched along the water's edge. Boats came and went on Mareotis carrying merchandise, olives, or the autumn vintage, and no storms troubled its placid surface so close to the sea and yet so safe. Little towns grew up on its shores, jetties invaded the water, and miniature harbours held harmless craft. The climate was delightful; tempering the summer heat and filling the sails the north breeze blew. Untroubled by frantic belief, unoppressed by excessive labour, the people of Mareotis prospered. They tended the vine, they sailed on the lake, and enjoyed in the course of their lives much tranquillity and pleasure.

Such an existence was too good to last. The Graeco-Roman period came to an end, and as the Roman machine ran down and its clockwork organization failed, Libyan barbarians broke in from the west. Their raids made life impossible and the lake-civilization decayed. At last an autumn came when the grapes remained unpicked, for the husbandmen had gone. Finally the flow of water from the Nile ceased and the lake itself disappeared.

Today on the ridges that once overlooked the water Beduin tents are pitched. On the site of vineyards they tend their goats and raise in a good season their sparse barley crops. Incurious they wander across the floor of an old harbour and shelter from the sun beside a ruined jetty. They see nothing of that past which for the visitor makes Mareotis one of the most moving places in Egypt. It is strange that mild, civilized, and unassuming husbandmen should have left as vital an imprint here as did in the Nile valley the powerful and assertive pharaohs.

The remains of the lake are now saline and the Beduin's first problem is lack of fresh water; but the ground is inexhaustibly fertile, and when winter brings a few hours' rain the spring hills are carpeted with wild flowers. Following the ridge which once dominated the lake, one drives through asphodel, iris, rock-rose, ranunculus, hyacinth, poppy, verbena, and seas of sweet-scented stock, marigolds, and ekium. The untended garden never ends; the scent is heavy, the colour bewildering. Scattered knee-deep among the flowers are the brown Beduin tents. Southward, where the sea breeze brings no moisture and rain rarely falls, the profusion dwindles, and at last passes into the bare yellow-grey Sahara.

Turning down to the basin of the ancient lake, one passes, where boats skimmed or tacked against the north breeze, into the harbour of Taposiris Magna, once the chief town of Mareotis. Though the spring tide in the harbour is only flowers, the dead place is remarkably alive, deserted yet remarkably peopled. On the basin no figure moves, yet there is a splash of oars and a bustle on the wharf. There is no sound but the hum of bees, yet voices echo over water. Dryshod one walks among anchor chains under the keels of riding ships. In the ruins of the town one looks repeatedly behind, embarrassed to trespass on so gentle and reasonable a people.

At the top of the slope that separates town and lake from the sea stands the ruined temple of Osiris where these people worshipped. Near by the broken signal-tower, once an exact replica of the great Pharos lighthouse but one-tenth the size, has weathered to ochre-yellow. Its rays no longer travel across the lake, and at night Taposiris is in darkness. Yet looking down from the flowered hilltop to where traffic once moved, the scene and the waterless basin are not desolate. The vintners' equable civilization has left something of its harmonious tempo. The husbandmen still animate the landscape. The life in Mareotis, though these Greeks never witnessed the festivals of Philadelphus or heard the quick wit of the museum's terracotta women, was not the least gift the Ptolemies gave to Egypt.

NINE

Cairo: The Great Medieval City

A first impression is the graceless impact of the 20th century. In a single generation the population of Cairo has trebled; the spacious green gardens and villas have disappeared; unkempt crowded streets are racked by the ceaseless blare of motor-horns; concrete blocks, rising in unplanned disarray, overshadow tenements. Yet from hotel windows, ten storeys up, the stranger glimpses to the east of the modern town a startling forest of minarets; on the street laden camels wait, with an air of disdain, for traffic lights to change; feluccas slip quietly downstream while cars and lorries roar across the Nile bridges; on the pavement by the river's edge, facing the high-rise blocks, men prostrate themselves at sunset towards Mecca; and, bound for Mecca, the Holy Carpet* sets out each year, not indeed with the Great Caravan as it did for seven centuries, but by aeroplane. Such inconsistencies betray the survival, amid the Westernizing present, of another city, the historic capital of Islam.

Cairo is still the first of medieval cities. For centuries it was immensely rich, and it was spared the Mongol invasion that destroyed the splendours of its rival, Baghdad. It remains a threatened but a miraculous survival, a blend of magnificence and squalor, extreme in its parade and poverty.

* See p. 131.

94

Though in the long span of Egyptian time it is a relative newcomer, its 2,000 years are richly recorded in its monuments. Neither Rome nor Istanbul offers a comparable architectural wealth deriving from the Middle Ages, and the old quarters of Cairo are perhaps less changed than those of any great capital.

Both history and monuments begin with Christianity and a Roman fortress. Egypt played a decisive role in the early development of Christianity. The cult of the resurrection associated with Osiris and with Isis, the Holy Mother, and her divine infant Horus, was easily assimilable to the new faith, and in a country notorious for its many astonishing beliefs the Romans were initially little concerned at the rapid spread of yet another religion. When a policy of repression was initiated towards the end of the 3rd century, it was too late. Tradition claims that 144,000 died in the persecutions of Decius and Diocletian, yet the church in Egypt stood firm. A hundred years later Christianity became the established religion of the country, and such it remained for over two and a half centuries. The temples were forcibly closed after 379 by the Edict of Theodosius, Emperor of Byzantium, and many were transformed into churches. On the walls of Philae beyond the Aswan cataract, the last stronghold of the Ancient Egyptian priesthood, were inscribed the words, 'The cross has conquered and will ever conquer.'

Yet to the alarm and disgust of Byzantium, the people of Egypt, as always idiosyncratic, began to insist on their own version of the imperial religion. They preferred to detect in Christ *one* nature in which the divine had absorbed the human, rather than the *two* natures, divine and human, separate but inseparable, that orthodoxy demanded. At the Council of Chalcedon in 451 their Monophysite doctrine was roundly condemned and thenceforward the majority of Egyptians were schismatics. The schism, product as much of national as religious feeling, reflected the opposition of native Egyptians, latent since Ptolemaic times, to all that emanated from Greece. For nearly 200 years, from Chalcedon to the Arab conquest in 641, there were two churches in bitter opposition: the official Orthodox or Melkite church, and the Monophysite or Coptic church enjoying the determined support of the greater part of the population.

The strategic Roman fortress of Babylon, south of the future site of Cairo, was the focus of a small port and town. It was of particular significance to the Egyptian Christians, for thereabouts the Holy Family was supposed to have settled after the Flight from Palestine. Today, within the ruinous fortifications that the Byzantines once garrisoned, six Coptic churches survive. It is a poor quarter, a maze of winding alleys, but it has perhaps been inhabited by Christians since St. Mark evangelized Egypt in the 1st century. Here Athanasius and the early Fathers may well have preached, and here Christian services were celebrated for centuries before the coming of Islam. The continuity is moving. Though the churches have been rebuilt and restored, the Monophysite rite they celebrate assumed its present form in the 5th century and has never changed.

The churches, of basilican type with triple apses (the latter having characteristic Roman tribunes), sometimes incorporate a curious feature: a returned aisle across the west end which seems to have served the purpose of an interior narthex. They are notable for their marble pulpits, and for the delicately carved ivory panels, characteristic of Coptic work, set in their wooden sanctuary screens. Examples of both date from the 9th to the 11th centuries. Of

17 Late pharaonic capitals, Temple of Edfu.

18 Medinet Habu. The descendants of those who built the temples labour today under archaeological masters to shore them up.

19 Alexandria Harbour. The Royal Harbour could berth, with the Harbour of Safe Return, 1,200 ships in Ptolemaic times.

20 Terracotta funerary figurine (3rd–2nd cent. B.C.), Alexandria Museum. Such terracottas are portraits of the ghosts that still seem to people the Ptolemaic city.

21 A citizen of Hellenistic Egypt.

22 Ibn Tulun Mosque, Cairo. The finest of congregational mosques achieves perfect rhythm and proportion.

23 The City of the Dead. Such stone domes are a distinguished feature of the Mameluke tombs.

24 Minarets of Sultan
Hasan, greatest of
Cairene *madrasahs*.

25 Turkish Baroque.

26 The desert monasteries of the Wadi Natrun saw the development of the
first Christian monastic rule.

27 The continuity is extraordinary: the black-robed monks of Egypt have been praying and planting gardens since the 4th century.

28 Apse of ruined Coptic convent: the 'White Monastery', Upper Egypt.

29 The black tents of the Beduin. Once enjoying the prestige of experts, they were the technicians of caravan transport.

30 A Sinai oasis: water, palms and a few tamarisks create shade and life.

31 Beduin women with their flock.

32 Vendors display their wares on the quaysides where the tourist
steamers anchor in their leisurely progress up the Nile.

greater antiquity is the crypt of the church of Abu Sargah which may antedate the 5th century. It is the simplest and perhaps the least vulgarized of the major shrines of primitive Christianity. The level of the surrounding land has risen some twenty feet, and according to venerable tradition the crypt marks the site of the house (then in the Jewish quarter of Babylon) where the Holy Family lodged during their stay in Egypt. Somewhere here Jesus as a child may have learned to talk—was it his parents' native Aramaic?—and to appraise the external world; here he may first have become aware of human relationships, relationships whose nature was so often to be profoundly modified by his teachings. In the Coptic Museum near by, fine woodwork, ivory carving, and early textiles, reveal that the distinctive and essentially religious art of the Copts, evolving from the Hellenistic tradition, was fully established by the middle of the 4th century. The Copts were to transmit both techniques and decorative motifs to the Muslims 300 years later.

The survival of the churches at Babylon (or Masr el-Qadim, 'Old Cairo', as it is now called) is perhaps less remarkable than the survival of the Copts themselves as a living community. They are yet another example of the stout resistance to change characteristic of the Nile valley from the earliest times. When Christianity after the Arab conquest disappeared elsewhere in North Africa, it persisted in Egypt, where the Copts maintained their faith in spite of hostility and intermittent persecution. Copts and Egyptians, initially synonymous, represented, when the Arabs arrived, all that remained of the civilization of the pharaohs and Ptolemies in Christianized form. *Qibt*, the Arabic name for the Copts, is the same as the word 'Egyptian', both deriving from the Greek *Aiguptios*.

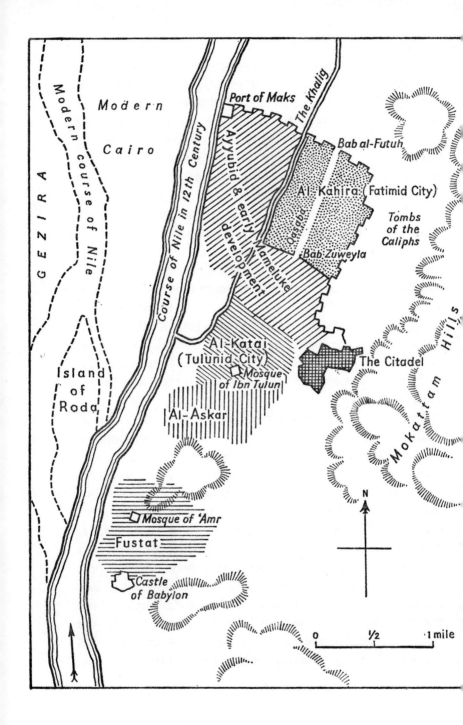

Modern Cairo

GEZIRA

Modern Course of Nile

Port of Maks

The Khalig

Course of Nile in 12th Century

Ayyubid & early Mameluke development

Bab al-Futuh

Al-Kahira (Fatimid City)

Qasaba

Tombs of the Caliphs

Bab Zuweyla

Island of Roda

Al-Katai (Tulunid City)

Mosque of Ibn Tulun

The Citadel

Al-Askar

Mokattam Hills

Mosque of 'Amr

Fustat

Castle of Babylon

N

0   ½   1 mile

Moreover, the blood of the Ancient Egyptians still runs in the veins of the religious minority that adheres to the Monophysite faith, for they have rarely married outside their church. At Babylon they maintained the Egyptian tongue until at least the 11th century, and it was still spoken in parts of Upper Egypt 200 or 300 years later. Today it survives in their liturgy though written in a script derived from Greek.

Subject to pressure over the centuries many Copts abandoned their beliefs, and through preference, indifference, or persecution, adopted Islam. The tenacious remnant, today somewhat over 5 per cent of the population, has thus survived a long and painful process of selection; it consists of men whose forebears were either clever enough to avoid persecution or brave enough to endure it, and for whom the appeal of Christianity was strong. The conditioning and intelligence of the Copts have for centuries tended to draw them into positions of importance. They have repeatedly been the treasurers, financiers, and advisers of their Muslim overlords, and in the 19th and 20th centuries their acumen brought many of them great wealth. At the same time the Copts have inevitably tended to develop the unattractive qualities characteristic of most oppressed minorities. It is not surprising that they have often been corrupt. Safety, let alone eminence, depended much on cunning, and their religion and society could only be maintained by a degree of subtlety and subservience. Such faults must be seen in the light of a religious constancy that is little short of heroic.

Alienated from their Byzantine rulers, the Christians of Babylon were not unduly distressed when the place fell to a small Arab force under 'Amr in 641. They may even have welcomed the commander's subsequent decision to establish the capital of a new Islamic Egypt immediately to the north. Built on the 'lines' (Latin, *fossa*) occupied by the attacking force in the course of the siege, it was called Fustat. Though containing the first mosque on Egyptian soil, the mosque of 'Amr, it was initially laid out as an encampment with separate quarters for each Arabian tribal levy. Later, developing into a considerable port, Fustat retained its primacy as a commercial centre until 1168 when it was fired on the approach of the Crusaders. The prize was denied the Franks, but the city that burnt for fifty-four days never recovered its prosperity.

Fustat was the first of five planned developments that contributed to the growth of the medieval city. All were set between the Mokattam hills and the lnie of the ancient canal that linked the Nile and the Red Sea (though the canal, known to the Muslims as the Khalig, was closed as an international waterway on grounds of policy in 765). As the prevailing wind across this sandy plain was from the Mediterranean, and successive rulers were intent to catch the cool summer breeze, the capital moved steadily northward until the end of the 12th century.

From 660 to 750 Egypt was a dependency of the attractive and informal Umayyad caliphs of Damascus, but when in 750 power and the caliphate passed to the Abbasid dynasty the country was controlled from Baghdad. The capital owed its next important extension to an Abbasid governor, Ibn Tulun, who established virtual independence in 870. He built north of Fustat (and also north of an intervening 8th-century development, al-'Askar, of which almost no trace remains) the new official quarter of al-Katai, with palace, government buildings, a hippodrome, and the famous mosque which bears his name. Ibn Tulun was a man of distinguished intelligence, learning, and character. His son

Khumaraweyh inherited his love of building but few of his other qualities, yet we owe to this fainéant an image that evokes the wealth and luxurious splendour of the Tulunid capital. Suffering from insomnia he laid out, in association with a palace that was greater than his father's, a pool of quicksilver surrounded by a loggia supported on silver columns; here, rocked on the softest of couches, he courted sleep guarded by a blue-eyed lion.

Some two generations after the insomnolent Khumaraweyh had met his death by assassination, the Fatimids of Tunisia arriving from the west, as few invaders have done, conquered Egypt. Like the Persians today, they were Shi'as, members of the heterodox sect of Islam that traces the descent of the caliphate through 'Ali, the murdered husband of the Prophet's daughter Fatima. Consequently Egypt became the seat of a Shi'a caliphate; it lasted 200 years and at the height of its power ruled from Tripoli to Damascus. To mark their conquest the Fatimids in 969 founded, north of Tulunid al-Katai which by then was largely ruinous, the royal quarter of al-Kahira, 'The Victorious'. Italian merchants corrupted the name to Cairo, though its native inhabitants have for centuries known it as Masr.

Laid out on a rectilinear plan, as Ptolemaic Alexandria had been, al-Kahira was an elaborate and ambitious creation. Its walls on the west bordered the Khalig canal and on the east overlooked the desert area known today as the City of the Dead (where the first notable buried was Badr al-Gamali, the vizier of Armenian birth who built the impressive gates of the Fatimid town). Al-Kahira was intersected from north to south by the wide Qasaba al-Kahira, flanked by the Greater and Lesser Palaces. The former covered seventy acres, and in the 11th century the palaces are said to have housed 12,000 domestics. Set in watered gardens were other royal pavilions: the pavilion of Emeralds, of the Zephyrs, of Victory, and (on the Khalig) the pavilions of Pearl and Gold. From grave and elegant mosques the Shi'a faith was disseminated. Ironically enough the mosque of al-Azhar, earliest of the Fatimid foundations, was to become in later centuries the most powerful theological college in Islam for the exposition of Sunni orthodoxy.

Like the earlier Tulunid capital, al-Kahira was an official precinct, the seat of military and civil government, but as the creation of an absolute caliph, who had nothing in common with the tradition of the desert Arab, it expressed a Byzantine formality and state. The commercial populace of Fustat required a permit to enter the walls; officials privileged to ride a horse could do so only at walking pace; and foreign ambassadors were obliged to present themselves modestly on foot. William of Tyre describing a Frankish embassy of 1167 conveys the imposing state that surrounded the Fatimid caliphs.

'Escorted by the vizier and his armed retinue through the subterranean passages that were a curious feature of the palace, the Franks passed through a succession of doorways, guarded by Ethiopian slaves, to find themselves in a courtyard paved with stone mosaic. Its marble columns supported loggias with fretted and gilded ceilings. Marble fishpools were filled with limpid waters, and they glimpsed exotic birds and strange beasts "such as the mind sees in dreams". As they approached the inner precincts of the palace they were awed and astonished by an increasing state and opulence. Pausing at last before the royal divan, the vizier thrice prostrated himself and removed his sword; then, as curtains embroidered with pearl and gold were drawn aside, the caliph was dramatically revealed, seated in regal state on a golden throne.'

The early Shi'a caliphs were as remarkable as their city. In their religious tolerance and width of interest, al-Mu'izz, the first Fatimid ruler of Egypt, and his son al-Aziz, call to mind the Emperor Frederick II 200 years later. Intelligent, sophisticated and highly informed, they were enlightened patrons of learning and the arts. The architecture, the pottery and textiles of their time are among the finest achievements of medieval Egypt. Their city also reflected immense wealth. The Caliph al-Aziz wore turbans of gold thread, and when he rode out, his jewelled harness was scented with ambergris and his stallions were clad in gold-inlaid armour. His sister, who died as an old princess in 1050, left 'besides many other objects, five sacks of emeralds, 3,000 chased and inlaid silver vessels, 30,000 pieces of Sicilian embroidery (probably mainly woven stuffs), and ninety ewers and basins of pure rock crystal'.* Even later, when the dynasty was in decline, the caliph boasted thirty-eight state barges, and his treasury included such exotic splendours as chess boards with gold and silver men, an antelope spotted with pearls, and a golden peacock with ruby eyes and feathers of enamel.

But from the end of the 11th century the Fatimids were under increasing pressure both from the orthodox (Sunni) caliphate of Baghdad and the Frankish kingdom of Jerusalem. Shortly after the arrival of the Crusader embassy described by William of Tyre came the burning of Fustat, and three years later in 1171 the great Saladin, acting in the name of the Abbasids of Baghdad, took al-Kahira. It was the end both of Fatimid rule and the Shi'a caliphate.

Recognizing no more than a nominal allegiance to

* Dorothea Russell, *Mediaeval Cairo*, London, 1962, p. 179.

Baghdad, Saladin was intent to secure the position of his own dynasty, the Ayyubids. Sunni orthodoxy replaced Shi'a belief, and the civil servants of the Fatimid regime were succeeded by a predominantly military administration. At the same time he took immediate measures to destroy the privileged character of al-Kahira, a symbol of Fatimid prestige. His officers were quartered in palaces and pavilions, merchants and refugees from Fustat were encouraged to settle within the walls. The royal enclave became a commercial centre. Buildings rose in the gardens, and the town soon lost its planned symmetrical character, becoming in due course the pulsing warren that we recognize today as an authentic remnant of the medieval city.

But like his powerful predecessors—'Amr, Ibn Tulun, and al-Mu'izz—Saladin made his own contribution as a builder. It was the last, and not the least imposing, of the planned extensions to the medieval city. Once again the new development was specifically designed as a royal and administrative quarter. With the eye of an experienced soldier, Saladin chose the elevation which we know as the Citadel, not far from the Mokattam hills and south-east of the Fatimid city. Begun in 1176, and surrounded with massive ashlar walls whose construction recalls the Crusader work with which Saladin was familiar in Syria, the Citadel became both a spacious fortress and a palace. Deep wells and elaborate waterworks made a garden of the arid hilltop and mosques rose within the walls. So well chosen was the site, and so secure its defences, that it remained the centre of government throughout the troubled centuries of Mameluke and Ottoman rule.

From 1252 when Saladin's dynasty collapsed, until the coming of the Turks in 1517, Egypt was controlled by

Mamelukes. Having more than a little in common with the *condottieri* flourishing in Europe, this military aristocracy was recruited mainly from Turcoman and Circassian slaves, born usually of Christian parents. They elevated sultans from among their number, and almost as often deposed or assassinated them. A semblance of legitimacy was conferred on these lawless rulers by the harmless existence in Cairo, from 1258, of the representative of the orthodox caliphate of Baghdad to whom they accorded a refuge without power. Though the Mameluke regime was bloody and chronically unstable, these professional soldiers drove the Franks from Palestine and repeatedly defeated the Mongols, thus ensuring that Cairo was spared the fate of Baghdad. They were also, strangely but fortunately for posterity, dedicated to building. Though they added no new and imposing quarter to the city, they crowded it with palaces, mosques, mausolea, hospitals, baths and caravanserais. These memorials to their power, wealth and ostentation, account for a majority of the architectural monuments that survive from medieval times.

The Mamelukes also threw up at intervals sultans of outstanding ability, both as soldiers and administrators. Many of the great names—Beybars, Kalaoun, an-Nasir, Kaytbay, el-Ghuri—are perpetuated in the monuments they built. The long rule of an-Nasir (1303–41), following the decisive defeat both of the Crusaders and the Mongols, marked the apogee of Mameluke Cairo. Egypt controlled the Levant ports, and the caravan traffic brought increasing wealth. The traveller Ibn Khaldun thus enthusiastically described the city some forty years after an-Nasir's death: 'I entered the universal metropolis, the garden of the world ... the gate of Islam, the throne of royalty, a city with embellished pavilions and palaces, endowed with conventual buildings and colleges, brilliant with the moon and stars of erudition.'

With the arrival of the Ottoman Turks in 1517 things changed decisively. The last Mameluke sultan, Tuman Bey, was crucified outside the Zuweyla gate of the old Fatimid quarter, and the last of the shadowy caliphs of Baghdad was spirited away to Constantinople. Egypt became a province of the Empire, and pashas appointed by the Porte were installed in the Citadel. The decline of Cairo over the next 300 years was rarely halted, but the blame must not be attributed wholly to Ottoman misrule. The discovery of the Cape route to India reduced the caravan trade which had long been vital to the economy of the city, and something like 10,000 riotous and oppressive Mamelukes troubled the capital and the Ottoman administration. In the circumstances it is astonishing that building continued, yet a notable legacy of the 17th and 18th centuries are the many elaborate marble *sebils* (fountains), which often add a baroque note to the medieval city.

Muhammad 'Ali Pasha symbolizes the 19th century. This capable Albanian made himself for all practical purposes independent of the Porte; disposed of the Mamelukes, cruelly but effectively; and initiated the growth of a Westernizing modern Cairo. Though in due course boulevards, such as Sharia el-Muski and Sharia Muhammad 'Ali, unsightly as surgical scars, sliced through the close irreplaceable tissue of the historic past, the major developments happily took place west of the medieval city, between the Khalig canal (that was filled in) and the Nile. At the same time the 19th century contributed a last element of architectural significance: the rococo palaces of khedives and pashas. In many ways suited both to Turkish taste and to the curvilinear tradition of arabesque, rococo found here, as it did on the shores of the Bosphorus, a last entertaining expression.

* * *

The great Islamic city, the nonpareil of the Middle Ages, whose development has been briefly traced, should properly have died long ago. Perhaps in any other country it would have done. Yet for all the pressures of the 20th century it still exists. In the area that was once the royal Fatimid enclave, and in the quarter to the south adjoining the mosque of Ibn Tulun, it is palpably alive. One has only to step into the side-streets and tortuous alleys to recognize a town which has here changed little since Lane graphically described it in his *Modern Egyptians* a century and a half ago. Of course there have been many alterations, not always for the better. But there is the same colour, sound, and movement, the same architectural splendour in profusion and decay. Sitting on his threshold a tailor is hunched over his needle, small shopkeepers drink Turkish coffee as they conduct unhurried business, a wrinkled hand emerging from an embroidered caftan raises a long pipe of cherrywood with an amber mouthpiece, a blind man stands beside a pile of hot loaves whose shape is of immemorial antiquity, the sherbet-seller passes clinking his metal cups, and black-robed women, now unveiled but still walking like statues, reveal the gleam of silver anklets. Supercilious camels transporting fodder, mounds of bright green clover, rock their way through the crowds, kites wheel in the blazing sky above, and sunlight strikes a hundred minarets and falls on half a million flat roofs. A hum rises from the throbbing fissures of the streets.

In such a setting the mosques convey a profound sense of

detachment; they are as withdrawn as those who enter to pray. The subdued tones of the masonry, the sense of time dripping like the water from the ablution fountains, repudiate the assertions of the street. Crossing these thresholds one steps into silence at a single pace. The empty court, the cool arcades, the sun and shadow, perhaps above all the space and simplicity of the early mosques, suit a noble conception of worship. The paraphernalia of many Christian churches seem fussy by comparison. Here are no family pews, no altars and no candlesticks, no pictures, no statues, no votive offerings. Music is superfluous where streets are never silent, and an escape from colour is welcome in a country where the sun always shines. The proportion and cool order of these mosques are an escape from noisy and crowded lives. The Muslim finds in these empty precincts the contrast that the Catholic peasant seeks in the glitter, warmth, and music of his cathedrals.

The Cairo mosques exemplify what may be called, for want of a better term, the classic tradition of Islamic architecture. It is a tradition that abhors the eccentric, the multifoil or the horseshoe arch, and the bulbous dome; it restrains, at any rate before the late Mameluke period, the tennency so often apparent in Arab art for meaningless convolution and debased arabesque. A satisfactory balance between plain and ornamented surfaces is scrupulously observed. For this reason those who have made acquaintance with Islamic art elsewhere, who associate it with restless complexity and trite elegance, are astonished by the dignity and simplicity of these medieval buildings.

It may be useful briefly to sketch their architectural evolution. When the Arabs arrived from the desert they had no architecture, and their characteristic style evolved through contact with two notable building traditions: the brick and stucco tradition of Mesopotamia and the ashlar tradition of northern Syria. They had, however, from the first their own ritual requirements, and these found architectural expression within a century of Muhammad's death in 632. Common to all mosques, these requirements include the *mihrāb*, a decorated niche indicating the direction of Mecca; the *minbar*, a pulpit possibly deriving from the churches of northern Syria; the *maksūra*, a railed enclosure designed to protect the caliph and later the imam when conducting prayers; the *dikka*, a platform on stilts whence the Koran is read and the imam's prayers are re-echoed to the congregation; a basin for ritual ablution; and finally the minaret, whence the muezzin, assuming the role once played by Muhammad's herald, summons to prayer.

Though incorporating such ritualistic features, the mosque, it must be emphasized, was never the dwelling place of the deity; it contains no sanctuary and is not served by a formal priesthood. Deriving from the courtyard of Muhammad's house at Medina where the Companions gathered for prayer, it is essentially a meeting place for the Faithful. The first mosques were in theory large enough to accommodate the whole local Muslim community.

Before the 16th century there were two main types of mosque, and both find their supreme exemplar in Cairo. The congregational mosques, the finest dating from the 9th to the 11th centuries, were essentially large arcaded courtyards. The arcades, usually arched, carried flat roofs on columns or piers. The arcades facing the Mecca or *kiblah* wall, four or more bays deep and always more numerous than those on the other sides of the court, sheltered the *mihrāb* (often preceded by a small dome), the *minbar, maksūra,* and *dikka.* The ablution fountain was placed for convenience in the centre of the courtyard, and a minaret or minarets usually at the end of the building farthest from the *kiblah*.

From the end of the 12th century, the congregational mosque tended to be replaced by the *madrasah* or teaching mosque. The latter, though often smaller, was highly sophisticated. The arcades of the congregational mosque disappeared to be replaced by four *eyvāns* or vaulted halls whose soaring arches gave on the courtyard. About the same time the external portal of the mosque became a prominent architectural feature, often flanked by twin minarets; and a domed mausoleum, usually that of the builder, was increasingly associated with the mosque. From the 14th century a further component—a fountain combined with a school for the teaching of the Koran (*sebīl* and *kuttāb*)—was frequently added to the complex.

The earliest Islamic building in Cairo, the mosque of the conqueror 'Amr at Fustat, once an evocative ruin, has been relentlessly restored. Thus an exploration of the Muslim architecture of Cairo logically begins with the 9th-century mosque of Ibn Tulun. It stands west of a municipalized open space that incongruously marks the site of Ibn Tulun's *meidān* and hippodrome, where 30,000 picked troops paraded and the Sultan played polo with his retinue. The mosque lies within a *ziyāda*, a protective enclave that is a rare feature associated with the earliest mosques. From the *ziyāda*, a doorway gives access to a vast arcaded court-yard. It covers six and a half acres. Piers with engaged colonnettes support the pointed arches of the arcades. On the *kiblah* (the Mecca side) the latter are five aisles deep, and two aisles deep on the other sides of the immense enclosure. Above the piers smaller relieving arches lend a sense of lightness and height to the arcades. Dating from 879, this is one of the earliest buildings to use the pointed arch throughout, and it here antedates the appearance of the Gothic arch in the West by two centuries. The builder, Ibn Tulun, came from Samarra, and the brick construction and stucco decoration speak of Mesopotamia, as does the stately minaret (rather later in date) which may well echo the design of the ancient ziggurats. There is little decoration beyond a fluent band of stylized floral stuccowork round the arcades, and internally a Cufic inscription in sycamore carried along the wooden coffered ceiling. From such simple elements this finest of congregational mosques achieves perfect rhythm and proportion. As often with great buildings there seems something inexplicable in its impact.

One other building in Cairo creates a comparable impression, the *madrasah* of Sultan Hasan. As Ibn Tulun is to lesser congregational mosques, so is Sultan Hasan to other *madrasahs*. Though built as late as 1356, when a certain decadence lay not far ahead, its virtues are firmly architectonic rather than decorative. The simple façade of the *madrasah*, rising sheer to a great height, is relieved by a powerful cornice and an immense stalactite-carved portal. Inside, a domed vestibule leads into a narrow passage that after a right-angled turn dramatically reveals the courtyard of the mosque from which rise with supreme confidence the soaring arches of the four *eyvāns*. As at Ibn Tulun there is a minimum of decoration; the bare walls rise skyward with immense effect.

Five hundred years separate Ibn Tulun and Sultan Hasan, but comparable architectural qualities find expression in many buildings of the intervening centuries, particularly those of the Fatimids and the earlier or Bahrite Mamelukes. As we have seen, the heterodox and talented Fatimids conquered Egypt a century after the building of Ibn Tulun and founded the new quarter of al-Kahira. Situated

on the line of an ancient caravan route, their remarkable
High Street, al-Qasaba (though now far narrower than it
once was) still runs from the Bab (Gate) Zuweyla to the
Bab al-Futuh. With great round arches and towers, these
imposing gates, surely the most splendid entrances to any
medieval city, were built towards the end of the 11th
century. Antedating Crusader influence, they are of
Byzantine inspiration. The Qasaba was for centuries the
primary thoroughfare of Cairo, and as such was repeatedly
enriched with fine buildings. The Fatimid palaces and
pavilions have gone, but beside their early arcaded mosques
—Salih Talaya, el-Aqmar, and the sombre ruin of el-Hakim
—rose in the 13th and 14th centuries the *madrasahs* and the
domed tombs of great Mamelukes—Kalaoun, an-Nasir, and
Barkuk. Nothing offers a juster impression of the splendours
of medieval Cairo than this historic thoroughfare.

A little east of the street lies the earliest Fatimid building,
the university mosque of al-Azhar founded in 970. Intended
initially to propagate the Shi'ite heresy of the Fatimids, it
became in 1171 the focus of orthodox Islamic thought and
learning. Subsequently its purposes and its syllabus under-
went little change for nearly 800 years. No society but that
of Islam could so have arrested the passage of time and
schooled the curiosity of men, preserving one world within
another. In this strange seminary, half-university and half-
church, many thousands of Muslims devoted themselves
from youth to memorizing the Koran and to the discussion
of the koranic commentaries. Often as many as half the
students were foreigners. From China, India, Malay,
Turkistan, and Morocco, the Faithful made their way,
often in the utmost poverty, to al-Azhar. There, where the
sun until yesterday went round the earth, they read the
unchanging texts of their predecessors, and studied to

become holy and learned men. Some of the advanced courses took half a lifetime to complete, but in the pursuit of spiritual truth years were of little significance.

In 1957 al-Azhar was partially secularized, and faculties of engineering, arts, medicine, and agriculture were added, perhaps unwisely, to traditional theological studies. However, one may still enter the vast paved arcaded quadrangle and find at almost any hour, sitting cross-legged upon their mats, solitary or in groups, theological students memorizing their Koran, with their shoes placed tidily beside them. As they learn by rote they sway backwards and forwards. Some of them will have been there since dawn and will have gone straight from the morning prayer to their book. Though most of them are poor, their circumstances are not necessarily difficult. Al-Azhar expresses the essentially democratic spirit of Islam. 'All believers are brothers', and students can usually obtain free instruction and housing through the religious endowments of the university. From the same source, millions of free loaves—20 million in 1929 —were at one time distributed to the students, and the rector of the university himself received 1,000 loaves a day in addition to his stipend.

Though architecturally al-Azhar has suffered much alteration, the simplicity of the 12th-century arcades where the students sit grouped on the ground about their teachers accords well with the spirit of asceticism. The shadows of pillars fall across tense preoccupied faces; the low repetitive chanting of a hundred passages from the Koran merges into a single sound; the rhythmic swaying never stops. Outside under the square of blue sky, figures wander in the sunlit court, and always somewhere, quietly and without self-consciousness, men prostrate themselves towards Mecca. For these students of theology, learning and religion are one.

Here are old men whose years have passed and whose skin has shrunk in acquiring their recondite knowledge. A commentary upon a commentary on one particular revelation of faith has filled their lives; a summer has passed computing the width of that tightrope which the Faithful after death must cross to enter heaven. Here if anywhere, before this negation of the flesh and devotion to scholarship, one can understand the spirit of the Middle Ages. Here is the lamp of the Schoolmen, and Grammarians' Funerals are everyday occurrences. Something in these courts compels respect.

Also in and about the Fatimid and Tulunid quarters survive the best examples of Islamic domestic architecture: private houses, baths and caravanserais, dating from the 14th century onward. The design of the private house altered little over the centuries. It presented a discreet exterior, and a bent entrance (such as those found in medieval castles) prevented any view of the interior from the street. The house, often several storeys high, was disposed round a courtyard with a loggia on one side, where a fountain induced cool during the long hot summer. The privacy of family life was the major consideration in the disposition of the rooms. Thus the *selāmlik* where the master received visitors was on the ground-floor, while the *harīm*, the women's quarter, was separately situated somewhere above. Additional privacy was ensured by wooden latticework windows, the *meshrabīya* grilles for which Cairo is famous. These, while admitting air and light, and providing a clear view of the street and courtyard, were impervious to prying eyes without. The chief rooms were often ornamented with a dado of coloured marbles, carved and painted ceilings, and the characteristic stalactite decoration of Islam. Divans, and many little cupboards, flush with the walls, largely replaced movable furniture. A number of these fine houses, though often much decayed, are intact; one or two, such as the Bayt el-Kiridliya adjoining the mosque of Ibn Tulun, are open to visitors.

Though any private house of consequence had its own bath or *hammām*, public baths were numerous. According to Makrizi, the 15th-century topographer of the city, there were forty-four in his day. One of the earliest survivals is the *hammām* built by the 14th-century Mameluke al-Mu'ayyad near the large mosque that bears his name. Such baths, reserved either for men or women, were places of social resort and played an agreeable role in Cairene life. Sometimes a group of women friends would hire a bath, installing themselves for the day with their slaves and singing girls. Massage and osteopathy were among the services provided, and the *hammām* combined for these female parties the functions of club and beauty parlour.*

As the terminus of great caravan routes and the resort of foreign merchants, the city was well endowed with caravanserais. There were still 200 in the middle of the 19th century. These 'inns of the East' were built round an open court and provided lock-ups and stabling for merchandise and beasts, with sleeping quarters for the merchants above. Though no longer serving their original purpose, and often much altered, there are survivals in the Fatimid quarter. Near the mosque of al-Azhar, the elaborately decorated 15th-century façade of the caravanserai of Kaytbay indicates, even though the rest of the building has largely disappeared, the care lavished on these establishments and how imposing the finest must once have been.

If the Fatimid quarter evokes the city's medieval archi-

* See Dorothea Russell, op. cit., p. 56.

tecture, it also provides an introduction to a merchant way of life that has persisted little changed in some of its *sūks* since the area first became a commercial centre in Saladin's time. As has always been customary in the markets of the East, each *sūk* or bazaar is reserved to a particular trade or the sale of a particular type of merchandise. This arrangement ensures, subject of course to formal bargaining between vendor and client, price control by competition between neighbours. Even the Khan Khalili, the tourist bazaar that lies a stone's throw from the Qasaba, has its interest. Though fine Egyptian antiquities, Coptic textiles, Fatimid pottery, and Persian miniatures have almost vanished from the Khan Khalili, the workmen, who sit hammering out the feeble brasses and finicky inlay that people seem ready to acquire, show the technical skill that has always characterized craftsmanship in the Nile valley. The goldsmiths' quarters near by have a more authentic air, and there one may find the richer fellah sensibly investing in a gold coin which traditionally will be added to the necklace securely strung round his wife's neck.

But it is the *attarine*, where spices are sold, that is truly compelling, and its streets are a reminder that the poorest Cairene wife understands more about spices than most Western cooks. One penetrates to this market by an alley so narrow that two can hardly walk abreast. Coverings are stretched above to exclude the sun, and one moves through a curious underwater twilight. On either side are piled sacks of rose-leaves, oregano, ginger, marjoram, mastic, cinnamon, saffron, and turmeric, twists of angelica, and jars of anise, cumin, cardamon, and sesame seed. The colours are pursed and dry, the textures sere. With mortar and pestle a perspiring boy is pounding some bitter root to fine dust. Here is everything that gives acuity to sensation or blurs the intractable moment; the scent that ravishes, the dram that sharpens a tiring appetite. Here, powdered and desiccated, are root, stem and leaf, half the green world. A rich, heavy indeterminate smell permeates the alleys; it is impossible to distinguish individual scents among all these dead fruits and flowers. The merchandise here, hardly changed since the 15th century, evokes spice-routes, caravans, and the aromatic cargoes of the Levant Company.

When Egypt in the 16th century was reduced to an Ottoman province, Cairene architecture, already in decline, came to reflect the taste of Istanbul. It sometimes did so with panache. Reference has been made to the baroque fountains of the 17th and 18th centuries, and to the stuccoed, marbled palaces of the khedives. The fountains, often associated with a *kuttāb*, are among the striking and decorative features of the old streets. Two or three adorn the Qasaba. Of the surprising establishments of pashas and khedives, many have disappeared, and the famous Bijou Palace on the Citadel suffered a disastrous fire. But at Shubra an entrancing summer pavilion still recalls the decadent glitter of khedivial rule. The suburb of Shubra was once the resort of grandees and foreign merchants, and the shady avenue that led there was crowded every evening with spanking equipages. In the seventies the sons of the khedive, each in a separate carriage preceded by four syces (outrunners), were the cynosure of this Rotten Row of the East. It was 'thronged every day from four to half-past six . . . elegant attachés on high-stepping Arabs . . . Jew bankers in unexceptionable phaetons, veiled hareems in London-built broughams, Italian shopkeepers in preposterously fashionable toilettes, grave sheykhs on magnificent Cairo asses, officers in frogged and braided frocks'.* Times

* Amelia Edwards, *A Thousand Miles up the Nile*, New York, 1877.

have changed. The avenue has disappeared, the ample garden surrounding the pavilion is neglected, and the pavilion itself is much decayed. Yet the building forcefully evokes the last splendours of the Turk before trim British administration came to herald the century of the machine.

The plain, rectangular, one-storeyed exterior gives no hint of the fantastic pleasance within. As the door opens, the interior provokes incredulous surprise. The scale is immense for such a toy. A loggia of white marble with slender arches surrounds what was once a sheet of clear water. In the centre is a marble balustraded island, supported on grinning crocodiles, where fountains played, and at each corner of the loggia an open marble kiosk of unusual delicacy curves into the lake. The way the loggia roof undulates over these kiosks is an architectural delight. Behind each kiosk lies a stuccoed and painted room, now dusty but unaltered since khedives entertained in this architectural fantasy a century ago. Ceilings and walls are covered with murals, apparently by Italian journeymen, set in giltwood or plaster frames. The decoration is wilfully eclectic. *Trompe-l'œil* curtains frame Tuscan landscapes. There are plump nudes, *capriccios*, grotesques and echoes of Pompeii, while in one room decorated with birds a bewildered ptarmigan rubs feathers with the birds of the Nile. This is not art and the execution is naïve, but these paintings, and those which liberally adorn the ceilings of the open kiosks and loggias, evoke with an almost painful nostalgia the delights and idle luxuries of a last rococo age.

Today clumps of rushes invade the sunken lake, black and white kingfishers dive into its stagnant waters, stone curlews nest on the loggia roof, and at twilight fruit-bats flicker in and out through paneless windows. Arabesque, allegory and landscape, flake from the walls; the marble revetments are loose. Yet built for pure pleasure this gilt and painted whim, a fretted frame for an artificial water, is still poised and self-assured. But unrepaired and unregarded, it can hardly last much longer. Like the khedivial society which once enlivened Shubra, it is out of fashion.

Perched on Saladin's Citadel, beside the undemonstrative 14th-century mosque of an-Nasir (a late and excellent example of the austere arcaded mosques that are the architectural delight of the city), stands the most familiar landmark in Cairo, the richly appointed 19th-century mosque of Muhammad 'Ali. Raised on the site of the Ayyubid palace where St. Francis of Assisi once preached to the Sultan al-Kamil, Saladin's nephew, it is, for its period, a building of unusual vigour. It is worth a visit both in its own right and for its terrace with the famous view. There at sunset the visitor should stand. A hum rises from the vast and diverse city below. Its buildings seem to pulse with the varied life they contain, and the narrow streets tunnel their way as through a comb of living matter. Beyond cupolas and minarets lies the modern town, paler in colour; then comes the Nile, and beyond skyscrapers and straggling suburbs the cultivation runs green to the horizon where the pyramids sit solidly on the desert edge as on a dais. Caught in the rays of the setting sun, dust is turned to gold and hangs like gauze over the city. Everything— past and present, mud-brick and concrete—is seen through this glinting haze which grows progressively more opaque. Then as the sun drops behind the Western Desert the haze vanishes. There is sudden twilight. In hot weather one can almost hear the city breathe its relief. Twilight deepens: mosques, minarets, and towering hotels are lost; finally even the Nile is untraceable. Pinpoints and scrawls of light are dotted and scratched upon a humming darkness that conceals a warren of 7 million people: the city of the Roman governors and the early Christians, of 'Amr the Conqueror, of the Fatimid caliphs, of Mamelukes and pashas; a city that officials, oilmen, entrepreneurs, businessmen, tourists and beggars, all share with the ghost of a sleepless Sultan rocked on a pool of mercury and guarded by a blue-eyed lion. The city indeed of the Arabian Nights.*

* Though the author of the *Arabian Nights' Entertainments* pretends to situate his stories in the Baghdad of Harun al-Rashid, the setting is in reality Cairo in the time of the Fatimids.

———◆•••◆———

TEN

Sands and Monasteries

The desert is Egypt's 'other' landscape. Unlike the cultivation, it is a landscape of hills and valleys, wind-eroded escarpments, and empty watercourses. On gravel wastes, flat as a billiard table, lie white curving dunes. It is a landscape of structural beauty, where neither flounces of vegetation nor man-made constructions obscure the geological rhythm, the statements of rock and strata, the terse articulation of ridges. There is nothing of the arrogant virility of growth. Whatever is green achieves life by licence of the drought, is small and self-effacing, survives between stones, thorny and abstract. It is landscape picked to the bone. Also, more than others, it is landscape that changes with the light. From dawn to noon it will shift through shadowy grey, pink, ochre, to blinding white, reversing the spectrum as the day declines. Except when choking sandstorms blow up from the south, the dry air is astringent and stimulating. The sun is eager, the nights bitter. The only sound is the wind.

This desert constitutes over 95 per cent of Egypt, but its character is markedly different west and east of the Nile. Stretching to the frontier—a straight line drawn by politicians through an empty Sahara—the Western Desert is little accidented, but it contains a succession of oases, strung out from Siwa in the north with the ruined temple of

Jupiter-Ammon to Kharga in the south. Situated below sea-level, the oases are fed by springs mysteriously deriving from the vast and distant swamps of the Sudan. The tops of waving palms, peering over the rim of these green depressions, herald villages, date groves, a remote economy. Though situated some 200 miles from the cultivation, and some of them beyond the high dunes of the Great Sand Sea, these oases support almost the whole population of the Western Desert, perhaps 150,000 people. Some, like Farafra, are pinpoints on the map, while the largest, Kharga, boasting a governorate and a railway, stretches ribbon-like for over 100 miles.

By contrast the smaller Eastern Desert, between the Nile and the Red Sea, is a tangle of hills, rising in places to over 7,000 feet. There are no great dunes or oases, but rains falling tens of thousands of years ago scoured deep eroded wadis, gorges of rock and shale. They hold the scattered wells that barely sustain a nomad existence. In these mountains, which still harbour ibex and a varied desert fauna, some of the animals associated with the grasslands that preceded the great desiccation found a last refuge. The 102 lions which a pharaoh of the New Kingdom, Amenophis III, claimed to have killed with his own hand were perhaps largely taken in the Eastern Desert. Where the tough landscape drops at last to the Red Sea, and handfuls of palms fringe the coast, are settlements, some of great antiquity dating from Dynastic and Ptolemaic times. Here the population, perhaps some 50,000, is concentrated. Throughout history they have been sailors and have fished off the coral reefs.

In the past the tourist sometimes ventured by camel to spend a night encamped beyond the Pyramids, but the deserts of Egypt until recently were reserved for the seasoned traveller. With his guides he penetrated after days on camel-back to the western oases or the Red Sea. But soon after 1920 came the first chugging motor, and mechanized explorers pushed into areas which had been the province of the camel. The car, more mobile than the caravan, was not tied to wells. Uncharted sandseas were crossed, and oases, lost since the days of the Roman camel corps, were reinstated on the map. With the Second World War, the Western Desert became a battleground and tanks churned it up. Machines have conquered the waste spaces, and now Everyman is a desert traveller. Egypt's second landscape is accessible. A notable but perhaps a sad change.

The Beduin driving his camels from one encampment to another, plodding by day through sun and sand, freezing at night, living as few other men could, sees a puff of dust on the horizon and halts his train. The dust approaches; perpetually scampering from its shadow a car comes into sight. Without hesitation the mite plunges into a wadi and with inhuman efficiency emerges at exactly the same speed. It is now close; the Beduin, screwing his glance into the sun, sees men with dark glasses and easy well-fed faces. They wave at his staring figure and he is lost, still motionless, in a cloud of dust. The hum of the engine dies away and in the stillness, uncomprehending and vaguely hostile, he jerks the head of his leading camel and the train hesitates into its slow swaying pace.

For the car-borne traveller, oppressed by over-civilization, the desert offers romantic escape. To brave its tempered difficulties gives him the same impression of being closer to life that some people get by sailing in open boats or climbing mountains. It is a common persuasion of those entering the desert that existence is more real 200 miles from water, with a rifle on the front seat and snake-serum in the duffel bag. Perhaps it is. The desert also offers a sense of imminent discovery. It is not the breathless suspense known to the explorer about to break upon a scene that has waited centuries for his arrival. Such an experience in ancient camel-plodded wastes is rare. Someone sometime has preceded the motorcar. It is precisely this that creates the possibility of discovery. The desert kills but does not destroy. Its rainless expanse preserves with painstaking care the memorials of every visit. In this undisturbed museum lies the wrack of the past: a Napoleonic musket, the overwhelmed caravan that a shifting dune reveals, or even that great cache which time may bring to light, the army of Cambyses lost on the route to Kharga. Time in the sand effaces little and its passage is difficult to detect. The stone cairn on the hilltop may have been raised yesterday or centuries ago. West of Qena, some miles off a caravan route, a human skeleton lies in the shade of a stunted thorn, the only tree in an endless landscape. Beside it is a half-buried wicker basket. Nothing indicates when the man died and whether by thirst or violence. Time offers no clues and only forbears to destroy. To windward, sand huddles against the bones.

The traveller can stop only for a moment's wonder. He must save his speculation and observe his itinerary. Time is water, and of that he carries only a few gallons. Stories about those who went out alone, broke an axle or sprang a petrol leak, are common; help came too late and they died of thirst. The driver cannot afford to linger over other people's skeletons. An inaccurate compass-bearing will not lead to the little three-star restaurant, or the hotel with a famous view. But the goal at the end of a long desert day seems more welcome than anything reached on a road.

The necessity to respect an exact time-table, to navigate with precision, is stimulating.

Though the traveller may establish intimacy with bits of this stark truthful landscape, the entirety escapes him. Behind the pyramids the desert stretches for 3,000 miles. The scale is not to be grasped. Words—immeasurable, illimitable—have little meaning. Strange that the traveller is often prompted to escape from the evening camp and his cars that huddle together for company, and to walk out of sight and earshot into oppressive silence, a silence so tangible it seems to pluck his sleeve. If he could stop breathing, still his rustling arteries and listen intently enough, something might change his life. Perhaps silence itself. But it is no use. With an idea of the intimacy of loneliness, he retraces his steps. About the camp, one corner of the desert is reassuringly human.

*   *   *

The motorist's predecessors, the historic inhabitants of the desert, are of two sorts, the sedentary monk and the wandering Beduin. Differing in race, religion, and way of life, they are a permanent commentary one on the other.

Deriving from a great ascetic impulse in the 3rd century, the Coptic monasteries of the desert occupy a unique place in the history of Christianity. The anchorites who combined to found them initiated a movement which was to inspire the monastic orders of the West, for the concept of monastic rule was Egypt's outstanding contribution to medieval civilization. Asceticism was no doubt a natural Christian reaction to the extreme hedonism of late Graeco-Roman Alexandria and the Delta towns. The dualistic view of things, to which asceticism relates, was familiar in Egypt, and some knowledge of earlier ascetic communities on the

Nile and in Palestine must have been current.* It needed only the persecution of Decian (A.D. 250) to prompt men to find safety and a vocation in the desert. Many of the early anchorites were simple peasants who believed, as do the fellahin today, that the desert is the natural home of demons (*afarat*). Retreat from the Nile was thus hardly a withdrawal; the ascetic carried the cross into enemy country.

The spread of anchoretic fervour was rapid and contagious, and it soon gained authority from a powerful name and personality: St. Antony the Great who removed to the desert in 285, and whose 'temptations' were to become a recurrent theme of Western painting. After initial hesitation the church supported the movement, and by the 4th century formal monastic communities were in being with legal status and power to hold property. Soon there were 5,000 monks west of the Delta; as a chronicler put it at the end of the century, *Quanti populi habentur in urbibus, tantae pene habentur in desertis multitudines monachorum*. Eastward the rule penetrated to Syria with St. Basil, and the authority of Athanasius established it in Rome. Martin of Tours carried the novelty across the Alps, and before long it reached Britain. No less than 2,000 monks were enrolled at Bangor, in northern Ireland. By 566 St. Columba was in Iona; Egyptian influence could go no further.

The monasticism of the desert was marked by an extreme severity and a purely devotional character. In such isolation there were few opportunities for education or good works. Thus the rule never exercised the same social influence as did the later orders in the West. As St. Jerome said, 'The

* This is Gibbon, terse and evocative, on the Essenes of Palestine: '. . . a solitary people who dwelt among the palm trees near the Dead Sea; who subsisted without money; who were propagated without women; and who derived from the disgust and repentance of mankind a perpetual supply of voluntary associates'. The Essenes disappeared two centuries before the rise of Christian monasticism.

duty of monks is not to teach but to weep.' The movement, enlisting chiefly the humble and uneducated, was essentially non-intellectual. Significantly our intellectual debt is to the hands rather than the minds of the desert fathers: in the best Egyptian tradition they were conscientious craftsmen and exact copyists. We owe to them many of the early Christian texts they faithfully transcribed.

The Egyptian monastic tradition has never been interrupted. A number of monasteries, such as the White and Red Monasteries at Sohag and the extensive ruined foundations of St. Simeon near Aswan, lie on the fringe of the Nile valley. But the tradition is at its most impressive in the true monasteries of the desert: St. Antony and St. Paul, isolated in the sere mountain landscape near the Red Sea; the four monasteries of the Wadi Natrun in the Western Desert; and St. Catharine in Sinai. St. Catharine, whose first patroness was St. Helena and whose monks claim privileges accorded by Muhammad himself, is the most famous foundation on Egyptian soil, but it is uncharacteristic in that the monks observe the Orthodox and not the Coptic rite. Unfortunately it is at present in Israeli hands and access from Egypt is impossible.

By contrast, since the construction of a road through the Western Desert to link Cairo and Alexandria, the churches of the Wadi Natrun, the most imposing testimony to Coptic monasticism, are within easy reach. The Wadi is a shallow depression, some seventy feet below sea-level; it holds a string of brackish lakes, and the natron they deposit was once used for mummification. The monasteries rise sombre above the depression and their high blank walls, incorporating a yet higher keep, have externally the air of fortresses. Security was vital, and until recent times visitors reached the gatehouse parapets by basket. Inside the walls are monastic churches (one at least dating in part from the 7th century), primitive refectories with long tables fashioned of adobe, ranges of cells, trees and shady gardens that surprise in this desert setting, and not least the sweet-water wells that made life possible.

An anchoretic settlement existed here as early as A.D. 330, and it was probably in the Wadi that the first formal monastic rule was established. The continuity is extraordinary, and a visitor to Egypt must see these strange survivals. He should do so soon. Within the last few years Deir Abu Makār, now ringed with concrete, has lost its ancient walls, and other architectural changes are disfiguring buildings untouched for over a thousand years. Deir Baramūs, the most remote of the four monasteries, is probably the least affected.

For centuries the concept of austere monks living the good life in this desert exerted a moral influence on the Christian world. Black-robed monks are still here, praying and planting gardens. Lineal descendants of the peasant saints, they offer the same simple hospitality to the curious visitor who comes to the Wadi as they did in early times. Though few of the monks are instructed, they believe that a richer life exists in the silence of the desert than in claustrophobic towns and the utilitarian landscape of the Nile.

*　　*　　*

With such a belief the Beduin, if they ever gave it thought, might agree. So linked are they to their wastes and nomadic rhythm that a long prison sentence is said to be equivalent to the death penalty. Freedom of movement is essential to them. It is the simple state of being to which they have long been conditioned, and which has become a physical necessity. Few peoples have been more romanticized than the Beduin, for those who come in contact with them begin by interpreting their life in terms of Western pre-conceptions. The camel-rider whom the stranger meets at sunset, with his hawk-nose and piercing eye, inlaid dagger-hilt protruding from his belt, swathed in all the associations of a burnous, is indeed an imposing and picturesque figure. Producing coffee in a black goat's-hair tent, two days by camel from the nearest water, his grace and hospitality enhance the impression. His endurance and his devotion to his desert are moving. But the desert is not the same to the Beduin as it is to others; for him it has no romantic overtones. It is simply the area where he scrapes an inadequate living amid intertribal feuds and tribal litigation. He has been outwitted in the struggle for sub-sistence and is left with the barren corners. Only his intense pride and the belief that he and his tribe are the salt of the earth reconcile him to his lot. Where there is no oil, he changes as little as his environment, and his evolution like the violent rains which once gnawed out the desert gorges occurred long ago. In the Eastern Desert, where a number of wells hold water throughout the year and there is a scant herbage in the deep wadis, some 6,000 true nomads survive. They do so with difficulty. In the Western Desert they are fewer, for most now, with an established foothold in the oases, have abandoned, except at certain seasons, the wandering life.

The status of the Beduin was once very different. Indis-pensable to a lucrative caravan trade, they were the techni-cians of the sands. Enjoying the prestige of experts, they provided both the navigational skill and the security essential to the successful transport of merchandise across the deserts. Though highly speculative, it was a trade that engaged great wealth and made great fortunes. With the arrival of the camel in Egypt in the 4th century B.C. desert transport assumed a new importance under the Ptolemies who fought repeatedly for the control of the camel routes; later the security of the *pax Romana* ensured the rise of caravan cities, flourishing desert entrepôts such as Petra and Palmyra. Medieval Cairo grew rich on the taxes derived from camel-borne traffic. Ultimately the exactions of the Mamekules in the 15th century raised the cost of spices in Cairo to five times that in Calcutta, thus prompting the Portuguese to seek, and open, a Cape route to India.

Across the Western Desert, from Assiut on the Nile, once or twice a year caravans of up to 2,000 camels set off down the Darb-el-Arba'in, the Road of Forty Days, for the distant oasis of Dafur, whence they returned with slaves, ivory, and the exotic merchandise of the south. Across the Eastern Desert, from Qena where the transit to the Red Sea ports was shortest, there was for long periods an almost constant traffic. In the 12th century Ibn Jubayr, poet and secretary to the Governor of Granada, travelling by this route to Mecca, said that the coming and going of merchant and pilgrim caravans rendered the desert 'animated and safe'.

But the major channel for the Egyptian caravan trade was the little Sinai desert, the bridge to Asia between the gulf of Suez and the gulf of Akaba. The Sinai mountains in the south, rising to over 8,500 feet, were known in dynastic times on account of their mineral wealth as the Turquoise Terraces. The rugged country holds dramatic wadis and small intimate oases, where water, palms and a few tamarisks create shade and life. The trees are full of birds, insects scud across a little pool, and the tension of the desert is relaxed. Here, on Gebel Musa, Moses is reputed to have received the tablets of the Law, and the Israelites may have found a refuge during their forty years in the Wilderness. But it was the undulating terrain of northern Sinai, between the mountains and the Mediterranean, that offered natural passage to caravans. Except during the Crusades, when the isthmus was intermittently closed, this strip of desert was for century after century an economic highway serviced by the Beduin. A northerly route through el-Arish on the coast led, via Damascus and Palmyra, to the Euphrates. As late as 1873, four years after the opening of the Suez canal, 1,358 caravans, large and small, passed through el-Arish.

A more southerly route, crossing the Sinai peninsula to Akaba and Petra, provided access to Arabia. This route was the famous Darb-el-Hagg, or Pilgrims' Road, the way both of commerce and the Faith. Here yearly crossed the gigantic concourse of beasts, men and merchandise that comprised the Great Caravan to Mecca. Assembling north of Cairo, sometimes as many as 50,000 persons, predominantly pilgrims, set out. They did so in two contingents; the second, composed of Berbers and others from the far west, had already travelled down the long North African coast. A day's march separated the contingents, and forty days brought those who did not succumb on the journey to their goal. With the caravan travelled two highly venerated objects: the Holy Carpet woven in Cairo as a covering for the Kaaba, the sacred stone at Mecca, and the Mahmal. The latter, an empty palanquin but the emblem of royalty, commemorated the litter in which the Sultana Shagar-ed-Durr had undertaken the laborious journey in 1272.

Where the Darb-el-Hagg crosses Sinai a little winter rain encourages, as on the Libyan littoral, sparse aromatic vegetation. In the spring there is a brief bright season of flowers, and sand-grouse nest on the gravel drifts. Here, through the treeless expanse, a dozen shallow but clearly defined troughs, perhaps eighteen inches wide, lead purposefully east. Each of them was trodden out centuries ago by the round leathery feet of camels picking their careful way across the desert. Swaying down these tracks, the major caravan route of medieval times, the laden files passed like armies on the march and the Beduin fulfilled their role in history. Few camels pass today. The abandoned tracks carry no pilgrims, spices, gold, leopard skins, or ostrich feathers. The Suez canal brought East and West too close. Ships spelt the finish of this ancient highway.

Though the deserts of Egypt still retain a remnant of Beduin and monks, survivals from the past, the commerce and the fervours of asceticism are history. Trailing their clouds of dust, the newcomers, the motormen, inherit the empty spaces. It is a little mournful.

ELEVEN

The Lords of the People

When the Egyptian, by one of the supreme efforts of history, emerged from a primitive twilight, evolving mathematics, instruments, organization, all that goes to make the beginning of a civilization, he embarked on the building of the pyramids. The Great Pyramid took 100,000 men twenty years to build, working during the months of the Nile flood. Though we are told that they were fed only on bread and radishes, this fantastic expenditure of labour would have exhausted a more developed economy than the nascent Nile state. The country could not afford the vital energy that went into these mountains of stone and the physical exhaustion that was the price of the building. On the decline of the Old Kingdom there followed 200 years of anarchy.

In the Middle Kingdom, with its semi-feudal organization, the governors and sub-governors of the pharaoh were probably more in touch with the people, and the government tended more to the general welfare of the country than at almost any period. But Amenemhet and Sesostris passed. With the coming of the New Kingdom, the pharaoh grew more a god and less a responsible ruler. Imperialism and theocracy pursued their own ends and the people were the losers. The story of the pyramids was repeated in a hundred temples, and the example of Cheops was handed on from dynasty to dynasty. While starving labourers threatened to storm the public granaries, the god Ammon, omnipotent and pampered, received 205,000 bushels of grain for the offerings at his annual feasts. Two thousand workmen, it is computed, were occupied for three years in carrying a single stone from Aswan to the Delta capital of Sais. Under Persian rule the labour of a city was devoted to keeping the wife of the satrap in shoes.

So the story went on. Often the country's worst enemies were its rulers. Pharaohs, military governors, Mamelukes, pashas repeatedly squandered the wealth and the lives of the people. When a pharaoh of the 26th Dynasty built the canal that was to link the Nile to the Red Sea, we are told that 120,000 men died. History repeated itself, and thousands more were dedicated to the triumphant passage of the Suez Canal. In their extremity the people vainly searched for leaders, seized on a Libyan saviour, Inaros who was crucified by the Persians, and later despairingly claimed that Alexander was a native Egyptian. In the Christian era, when they found a Coptic patriarch to represent them, they were ready to outface the Emperor of Byzantium.

An intelligent Ptolemy, a clement proconsul, or a shrewd caliph, might ensure interludes of wise government, but Greek, Roman, and Arab passed, while the countryside continued to belie the promise of its labour, its rich water, and richer soil. The bitterest draught was reserved for the last. To confound matters utterly came Ottoman rule in 1517. Until Napoleon landed nearly 300 years later, Egypt progressively declined. The country became a province whose interest for the government lay in its capacity to produce revenue. But the more Egypt was squeezed, the less there was to give. Canals went out of use, irrigation and crops were uncertain, the population fell. It was the same with education. Whereas fifty years before the

Ottoman conquest there had been 155 schools in Cairo alone, at the beginning of the 19th century there were fifteen in all Egypt.

On the departure of the French, Muhammad 'Ali, 'the founder of modern Egypt', manœuvred, fought, and murdered his way to power. He was undoubtedly a great figure, and certainly a great benefactor to the country. He restored order, reorganized the economy, and launched agricultural and educational reforms. But though he virtually emancipated Egypt from the Sultan, it was in fact a Turkish government and Turks who remained in power. Muhammad 'Ali was an Albanian, spoke no Arabic, and the only theory of government he recognized was that of the Sublime Porte. He differed in that his practice was more efficient, and that he had a wider vision. He replaced a bad Ottoman rule by a relatively good one. The army, officered by Turks and Syrians, continued to be drilled in Turkish until after the First World War. Prior to a rising in the early 1880s probably only a handful of true Egyptians penetrated into the ranks of society, although a number of influential families exercised a delegated power in the provinces as intermediaries between the rulers and the people. Meanwhile the ruling caste continued to be largely supplemented, in traditional Ottoman fashion, by emancipated slaves. As late as 1855, the Governor of Cairo, the Minister of Finance, the Minister of Police, and Zulficar Pasha, one of the most important men of the time, rose to office from slavery. This habit of elevating the private servant to the public ministry, and the dependence of office upon intrigue and the whim of an absolute ruler, were not conducive to forming what Egypt needed most at that time, a responsible aristocracy. Neither was the form or intention of the government calculated to supply a want which Egypt was to feel even more in the 20th century, an enlightened, independent, and active middle class. Lastly, the backbone of the country, the fellahin, felt no identity with the state that Muhammad 'Ali created, and could not be expected to do so. They resented conscription by an alien government; the traditional, almost mystical, obstinacy of the fellahin led them to prefer self-mutilation to service. They were circumvented by the cunning of Abbas I; with almost equal obstinacy he formed two battalions from men lacking an eye or a trigger-finger.

It is not surprising that the refrains of the fellahin at this period were strongly anti-authoritarian. Two-part songs such as the following were symptomatic of their feelings:

A: They starve us, they starve us,
B: They beat us, they beat us,
A: But there's someone above,
   There's someone above,
B: Who will punish them well,
   Who will punish them well.

Muhammad 'Ali believed that within ten years of his death his family would be driven from the throne. Such was not the case, and the old man's foresight for once was wrong. His death in 1849 was followed by a period of family rule whose inefficiency undid much of the good that he had achieved, retarding the development of the country for another half-century. Education languished, or advanced by fits and starts; Muhammad 'Ali's School of Languages became Shepheard's Hotel and Mr Shepheard's waiters succeeded to the professors of English, French and Oriental languages. Corruption flourished, government was capricious, and there was little incentive for private enterprise. A provincial governor who barbarously tortured fellahin to encourage the payment of taxes, when charged with the practice naïvely replied that he had given it up because it did not pay. Officials could hardly be expected to preserve a standard of moderation, having continually before them the example of the palace. Though a capable ruler and a talented soldier, Ibrahim Pasha had so gargantuan a thirst that he succumbed on a hot day to the effects of two bottles of iced champagne drunk at a sitting. His successor Abbas I was a notable orgiast; like his pharaonic predecessors 3,000 years earlier, he kept and consulted magicians and astrologers. Next in the line, Said, with a reputation for jovial good humour, is said to have blown recalcitrant Beduin from the muzzles of his guns. The Khedive Ismail was a sympathetic character but hardly more gifted in the art of government. His laudable schemes for education and social services went awry, and before his abdication in 1879 his extravagance had run the country deeply into debt. It was particularly unfortunate that after Egypt first came in contact with the mechanical civilization of the 19th century it should, for nearly fifty years, have been subject to inept rule.

Before the departure of Ismail the British and French had assumed control to protect their financial interests and avert the bankruptcy of the country. Not long after came British occupation. For the fellah this was simply a change of foreign masters. The British, like their predecessors, were in Egypt for their own reasons, and with little more excuse. But there was this important difference: the recovery of Britain's financial stake in the country depended on a measure of prosperity. Egypt was greatly in need of that organization, easily available justice, and lack of corruption, which followed. For these reasons the Occupation, until the First World War, represented for the fellah a more acceptable form of government.

However, the lasting importance of the Occupation was the spirit of nationalism it provoked. It could be said that the most valuable contribution of British rule was the corporate resentment it ultimately aroused. The man at the *shadūf* and behind the plough stirred. A word went round and a people woke to political consciousness. Under Muslim overlords, under rulers of the same colour and belief, national feeling might never have touched the man in the field and the street; Ottoman absolutism, and the exclusion of the true Egyptian from public life and office, might have continued for decades. Once nationalism had grown vigorous, it was inevitable that native Egyptians should be drawn into positions of responsibility. The fellah, though still the beast of burden that carried the weight of the country, was at least incorporated into the household. A nation was created where had formerly been a collection of persons.

The departure of the British left Egypt for a time subject to the caprice of an injudicious and misguided monarch. In 1952 he also went. Perhaps then Muhammad 'Ali's modern Egypt came of age. For the first time there was something like identity of interest between the rulers and the ruled. A new generation has seen radical social and educational changes, the wholesale reform of land tenure, and ambitious irrigation schemes. In some twenty years much has been achieved.

Few leaders have been confronted with as difficult a task as Nasser and his successors. The country suffers war, or a virtual state of war, that is likely to be long drawn out. This calls for an expenditure on armaments that can be ill afforded but cannot be reduced. At the same time the population is increasing at a rate that unless halted will spell disaster; the demographic problem is immediate and of fearful gravity. Not least, the material values of the West that find an enthusiastic welcome in Egypt, when they are increasingly questioned in Europe, threaten the very basis of Islamic society.

But there is reason to hope. A great fund of character and vitality resides somewhere in this ancient people. In a country where there was never a caste system even in pharaonic times, a new corporate identity comes naturally. Given a rule they respect the fellahin and their river are capable of untold achievement. A long historical hibernation, which proved impervious to the passage of dynasties and the pressures of imperial policy, seems to have reached its term. The Egyptian is perhaps aware that an inheritance awaits him. After all this time, he deserves it.

Brief Chronology

————◆••◆◆————

ANCIENT EGYPT

c. 3000–2680 *Early Dynastic Period:* unification of Upper and Lower Egypt; tombs of 1st and 2nd Dynasties at Abydos and Memphis.

c. 2680–2200 *Old Kingdom:* 3rd to 8th Dynasties; capital at Memphis; the age of the pyramid builders.

c. 2000–1670 *Middle Kingdom:* reunification under 12th and 13th Dynasties; capital at Thebes and Fayum; conquest of Nubia.

c. 1570–1085 *New Kingdom:* 18th to 20th Dynasties; the imperial age; Asiatic conquests; vast wealth reflected in splendours of Thebes; growing power of the priesthood.
(Mid 14th century, Akenaton briefly establishes monotheism at Amarna.)

c. 1085–332 *Late Kingdom:* Egypt recurrently the prize of foreign rulers; high priests as pharaohs (21st Dynasty); Libyans as pharaohs (22nd and 23rd Dynasties); Ethiopians as pharaohs (25th Dynasty).

663–525 Florescence of the archaizing Saite (26th) Dynasty. Conquest of Egypt by Cambyses, followed by repeated struggles to throw off Persian rule.

THE PTOLEMIES

332 Arrival of Alexander the Great.

323–221 Alexandria, the new capital, flourishes under the first three Ptolemies.

150–30 Increasing Roman pressure; death of Cleopatra; Egypt annexed as an imperial province.

THE ROMANO-BYZANTINE PROVINCE

1st century St. Mark founds the church of Alexandria.

141

3rd century	Persecutions of Decius and Diocletian; tradition of desert monasticism develops.
4th century	Christianity becomes state religion, but Egypt torn for 300 years by religious controversy.
c. 326–73	Athanasius, patriarch of Alexandria, leads struggle against the Arian heresy.
389	Emperor Theodosius closes the pagan temples.
444	Patriarch Dioscurus firmly supports the Monophysite doctrine.
451	Monophysite doctrine, to which Egypt remains passionately attached, condemned at the Council of Chalcedon.
451–641	Increasing Byzantine oppression of the Monophysite church alienates the population, who offer little opposition on the arrival of the Arabs in the 7th century.

MEDIEVAL AND OTTOMAN EGYPT

632	Death of Muhammad.
641–2	'Amr, acting for the Caliph 'Omar, second in line from the Prophet, conquers Egypt, builds the mosque of 'Amr.
661–750	Governors representing the Umayyad caliphs of Damascus.
750–868	Governors representing the Abbasid caliphs of Baghdad.
868–969	Tulunid and Ikshid dynasties establish virtual independence of Baghdad; building of al-Katai and mosque of Ibn Tulun.
969–1171	Fatimid conquest and building of al-Kahira. Egypt the seat of a heterodox Shi'a caliphate; first Crusader invasion.
1171–1252	Saladin and the Ayyubid Dynasty, recognizing no more than the token authority of the last caliphs of Baghdad. Egypt reverts to religious orthodoxy; building of the Citadel and walls of Cairo.
1252–1382	Bahrite Mamelukes; Crusaders driven out of Palestine and repulsion of the Mongols; Cairo becomes a 'city of domes', thanks to the great tomb-builders: Beybars, Kalaoun, an-Nasir, Sultan Hasan, and others.

1382–1517   Circassian Mamelukes; defeat Tamerlane; last architectural masterpieces of medieval Cairo, the work of builders such as Kaytbay and al-Ghuri.

1517   Selim I conquers Egypt which becomes a province of the Ottoman Empire.

MODERN EGYPT

1798–1801   Bonaparte's Expedition.

1802–49   Rule of Muhammad 'Ali Pasha. (Acknowledging only the formal suzerainty of the Porte, he begins the modernization of the country.)

1876   Financial chaos and the imposition of Anglo-French fiscal control.

1882–1922   British Occupation and Protectorate.

1922–52   Kingdom of Egypt. (The Sultan ascends the throne as King Fuad I, and is succeeded in 1937 by King Farouk.)

1952–3   Military *coup d'état*, abdication of King Farouk, and establishment of the Egyptian Republic.

1956–70   Presidency of Gamal Abdel Nasser.

1970–   Anwar Sadat succeeds to the Presidency.

Notes for the Traveller

3. THE VALLEY LANDSCAPE

With the exception of the strange swamp lakes, such as Burullus and Manzala, bordering the sea near the mouths of the Nile, the scenery of the Delta is the most uniform, and usually the least interesting, in the country.

The valley landscape is particularly attractive 'betwixt the desert and the sown'. Here on the fringes of the cultivation are small pools and brackish waters. They are sometimes alive with wildfowl, for during the spring and autumn migrations the valley is one of the world's great channels of passage. (Ornithologists are well served by *The Birds of Britain and Europe with North Africa*, a Collins paperback, and even better by Meinertzhagen's two folio volumes *The Birds of Egypt*.)

Lake Karoun and the Fayum 'Oasis' (eighty-five kilometres south of Cairo) present a character of their own. There is a good road, and a couple of less good inns on the lake. The latter (flamingos and a quantity of wildfowl), lying between the desert and the cultivation, is of great beauty, particularly at dawn and sunset. A visitor should cross the lake by rowing-boat and walk to the Ptolemaic temple that stands in the isolation of the desert: an unforgettable experience. The Oasis itself is notable for its luxuriance, its decorative dovecots, its little canyons and hurrying waters, the last two a great contrast to the usual landscape of the Nile valley. That distinctive bird, the Senegal Coucal, is common in the area.

4. THE DWELLERS ON THE LAND

No just estimate of the people is to be derived from the villages where tourists resort, such as those near Memphis, Abydos or Luxor. The touting and the importunities met with in such places are uncharacteristic. The charm, the humour and the dignity, of the fellahin will be found elsewhere. Best go with an Egyptian acquaintance to areas where a European face is unfamiliar. It will be a rewarding experience.

7. THINGS MADE WITH HANDS

Pharaonic architecture begins at Sakkara (thirty-three kilometres south of Cairo) with Zoser's vast funerary complex of which his Step Pyramid is the focal point. Here, dating from the 28th century B.C., is the first major ashlar building in the world, the earliest engaged column, the earliest capital. The work exhibits an astonishing restraint and elegance.

Painted bas-reliefs, which are perhaps the supreme artistic achievement of Ancient Egypt, also begin in the extensive necropolis at Sakkara. Here in the tombs of the court dignitaries (e.g. tomb of Ti, tomb of Mereruka) are to be found the linear eloquence and sophistication that recur a thousand years later in the Tombs of the Nobles at Thebes (e.g. tombs of Nakht, Menna, and Ramose). In the matter of vitality the bas-reliefs of the pharaohs rarely compare with those of their servitors.

A century after the Step Pyramid came the pyramids of Giza. Presumably no one visiting Cairo fails to see them or Kephren's mortuary temple (the sole survivor of the valley temples originally associated with the pyramids). There are, however, some two dozen pyramids, dating mainly from the Old Kingdom (2780–2300 B.C.), scattered along the edge of the Western Desert southward from Cairo. Some are little visited and make a more agreeable impact than the busy pyramids of Giza. The finest perhaps are those at Maydum and Dashur.

To travel south to Luxor is to move from the Old Kingdom to the imperial phase of Egyptian history (1570–1085), from the pyramid to the rock-hewn tomb, from the chaste simplicity of Sakkara to the grandiose cult and funerary temples of Thebes. New features appear: processional sphinx avenues, massive pylon gateways, colossal statuary, red granite obelisks. The emphasis is on size, yet the immensely wealthy and compulsive builders of the New Kingdom produced a number of monuments distinguished for their purely architectural qualities. Among such are the forecourt of Amenophis III in the temple of Ammon at Luxor, Hatshepsut's elegant and revolutionary temple at Deir el-Bahri, the hypostyle hall of the Ramesseum at Thebes, the temple of Seti I at Abydos, and not least the little temple of Ptah at Karnak (restored in Ptolemaic times) where a single ray of light dramatically illuminates the statue of the goddess Sekhmet.

The function and layout of the Egyptian temple, which persisted virtually unchanged from the New Kingdom to the Christian era, are best understood in the later Ptolemaic buildings. Edfu, half-way between Luxor and Aswan, demonstrates clearly in its remarkable state of preservation such features as the axial planning of the temples (the progress through the forbidding pylon to the open forecourt, thence to the claustrophobic hypostyle, and finally to the obscure and narrow sanctuary).

The Egyptian Museum in Cairo offers a commentary on three millennia of pharaonic civilization. Haphazard, cluttered, grubby, it has a charm lacking in many aseptic and well-ordered collections. Though the average visitor will probably go first to the Tutankhamun exhibits, it is the objects of the Akhenaton period from Tell el-Amarna that are likely to make the greatest impact. Hardly less striking are many of the statues of the Middle Kingdom, while the naturalistic portraiture of non-royal persons is often notably good throughout the pharaonic period. From the pre-dynastic vases onward, the Museum reveals the Egyptian craftsman's continuing sensitivity to materials.

8. THE CITY OF ALEXANDER

Alexandria has never been systematically excavated. Pompey's Pillar; the theatre, street, and baths recently revealed; the site of the Pharos; the Museum of Antiquities: these must be visited. They evoke but a fraction of the Hellenistic city. Imagination must create the rest with the help of the blue waves creaming in the bays, the shallow waters of Lake Mariout with their birds and their melancholy black fishing-craft, and the spring flowers that cover the lost vineyards of Mareotis. To find a flowered littoral and warm beaches, a visit to Alexandria should be timed for late spring or early summer. There is little to recommend it in winter.

9. CAIRO: THE GREAT MEDIEVAL CITY

The itineraries in Dorothea Russell's *Mediaeval Cairo*, reflecting the researches of K. A. C. Creswell and other authorities, offer the best practical guide to the city. There is a vast amount to see; the following is a brief selection.

Christian Antiquities. In Old Cairo (Masr el-Atika), the Coptic quarter and churches, notably St. Sergius, St. Barbara, and Mu'allaqa.

The Coptic Museum houses a collection of early Christian art (woodwork and textiles of special significance).

Early Muslim. Mosque of 'Amr, Nilometer, mosque of Ibn Tulun.

Fatimid Period. Gates of the Fatimid city; the following mosques and tombs: al-Azhar, al-Guyashi (on the Mokattam hills above the citadel), el-Hakim, al-Gafari, al-Aqmar, Saiyida 'Atika, Saiyida Ruqayya, As-Salah Tala'i. All these buildings, except the last, date from before the middle of the 12th century.

Ayyubid and Mameluke Periods. The wealth of monuments grows bewildering. A selection must include Saladin's Citadel, with the 14th-century mosque of an-Nasir; Tombs of the Caliphs (notably Barkuk, Barsbay, and Kaytbay); the mosques or *madrasahs* of Sultan Hasan, Sarghatmish, Kaytbay, the 'Blue Mosque', Imam Shafi'i, al-Maridani, el-Mu'ayyad, el-Ghuri, Kalaoun, an-Nasir, Barkuk (the last five in the Qasaba quarter, as is the 14th-century palace of 'Uthman Katkhuda); and the curious 14th-century foundation of the Bektashi dervishes tucked into the cliffs of the Mokattam hills.

The Turkish Period is well represented by numerous baroque fountains, by Muhammad 'Ali's mosque on the Citadel, and by the decayed splendours of Shubra Palace. Amateurs of Edwardian architecture should not miss Heliopolis (much that is curious, not least the palace modelled by Baron Empain on Angkor).

The Museum of Islamic Art does for medieval Cairo what the Egyptian Museum does for Ancient Egypt. See especially the Tulunid and Fatimid work (frieze from the vanished Fatimid palace); fine inlaid metalwork, chiefly of the Mameluke period; unique collection of enamelled glass mosque-lamps.

If the chance occurs to visit the medieval city on the occasion of one of the major religious festivals, such as the *mūlid* of Saiyida Zenab or the Birthday of the Prophet, it should on no account be missed.

10. SANDS AND MONASTERIES

Though the motorist has inherited the desert, it remains unwise to venture more than a few miles out except with *two* cars equipped with appropriate tyres and sun-compass. If a motorist is more than a day's *walk* from a metalled road, a breakdown in a single car, or the close embrace of a sand-dune, may be a serious matter.

An arm of the Great Sand Sea intrudes between the Nile valley and the oasis of Baharia, two or three hours' drive from Cairo. These majestic Saharan dunes are beautiful and imposing.

The strikingly different character of the Eastern Desert, with its wells and gorges, can be appraised south of the capital. The Wadi Digla is accessible from Meadi (thirteen kilometres from Cairo), where there is also a petrified forest, and the Wadi Hof from Heluan (thirty-five kilometres). Both are dramatic. In the region of the Wadi Rish-Rash, somewhat farther south, there are ibex.

The Wadi Natrun, easily visited from the desert road that links Cairo and Alexandria, best evokes the unbroken tradition of Coptic monasticism. But there are monasteries, many of them ruinous, on the desert fringes all up the Nile valley. Dating from the 4th century the White and Red Monasteries near Sohag, between Assiut and Luxor, are among the most important. The ruins of the vast monastery of St. Simeon lie in the desert only two kilometres west of Aswan.

Books

---

1. THE COUNTRY AND THE TRAVELLER

The *Guide Bleu* is the best of the handbooks. For Ancient Egypt it may be usefully supplemented by G. Posener, *Dictionary of Egyptian Civilization*, 1962. In Egypt from August to November, *c.* 450 B.C., Herodotus (*History*, vol. i, Everyman) is the most informative of the early visitors. For more recent impressions see J.-M. Carré, *Voyageurs et Ecrivains Français en Egypte* (2 vols., Cairo, 1932), and the select bibliography in *English Travellers in the Near East* by Robin Fedden ('Writers and their Work', No. 97, British Council, 1958). Gustave Flaubert's *Notes de Voyage* (in Egypt 1850), and Lady Duff Gordon's *Letters from Egypt* (1862–9), indicate how good the travellers can be.

2. THE ORGANIZED OASIS

Hermann Kees, *Ancient Egypt, a Cultural Topography*, 1961.
Michael Grant, *The Ancient Mediterranean*, 1969.

4. and 5. THE DWELLERS ON THE LAND; LIFE IN THE VILLAGE

W. S. Blackman, *The Fellahin of Upper Egypt*, 1927.
Amir Boktor, *School and Society in the Valley of the Nile.*

7. THINGS MADE WITH HANDS

L. M. Phillipps, *The Works of Man* (reprinted 1932), offers a critical, perhaps over-critical, assessment of the art and architecture. S. Giedion, *The Eternal Present*, vol. ii ('The Beginnings of Architecture'), 1964, is original and stimulating. J. M. White, *Everyday Life in Ancient Egypt*, 1963, provides an insight into both the life and thought of the Dynastic Period. See also A. M. Badawy, *A History of Egyptian Architecture* ('The Middle Kingdom', etc., 1966; 'The Empire', 1968), and standard works such as Stevenson Smith, *Art and Architecture of Ancient Egypt*, 1958.

8. THE CITY OF ALEXANDER

For a concise appreciation of Ptolemaic Alexandria, E. M. Forster's *Alexandria: a History and a Guide*, Alexandria, 1938, is unrivalled. A. de Cosson, *Mareotis*, 1935, evokes the life of the vanished lakeside society of Mareotis. See also H. I. Bell, *Egypt from Alexandria the Great to the Arab Conquest*, 1948, and J. Marlowe, *The Golden Age of Alexandria*, 1971.

9. CAIRO: THE GREAT MEDIEVAL CITY

Marcel Clerget's two volumes, *Le Caire, Etude de Geographie Urbaine et d'Histoire Economique*, Cairo, 1934, are a key work for the topographical and economic development of the medieval city; S. Lane-Poole, *The Story of Cairo* (Mediaeval Towns Series), 1906, agreeably covers much of the same ground. For the continuing flavour of the city, read E. W. Lane, *Account of the Manners and Customs of the Modern Egyptians* (Everyman). For Christian Egypt, see E. L. Butcher, *The Story of the Church in Egypt*, 2 vols., 1897, and E. R. Hardy, *Christian Egypt*, New York, 1952. For the Islamic monuments, see K. A. C. Creswell, *A Short Account of Early Muslim Architecture*, 1968, and his *Muslim Architecture in Egypt*, 2 vols., 1952 and 1960, and E. T. Richmond, *Moslem Architecture*, 1926. The best working guide for the visitor is Dorothea Russell, *Mediaeval Cairo*, 1962, but Mrs. R. L. Devonshire's books (*Rambles in Cairo* 1920, and, especially, *Some Cairo Mosques and their Founders*, 1921) are still useful.

10. SANDS AND MONASTERIES

The fierce spirit and loving-kindness of the early ascetics are evoked in *The Desert Fathers*, 1936 (Helen Waddell's commentary and translations from the *Vitae Patrum*): a necessary corrective to the scoldings of Gibbon and Lecky. For the Wadi Natrun, see Robert Curzon, *Visits to Monasteries in the Levant* (reprinted 1955), and Dorothea Russell, *Mediaeval Cairo* (Chapter 18, 'The Monasteries of the Wadi Natrun'), 1962.

M. Rostovtzev, *Caravan Cities*, 1932, gives a good idea of the volume and importance of the caravan trade in the first centuries of our era.

A. C. Wood, *History of the Levant Company*, 1935, reflects the decline after the opening of the Cape route to India. C. S. Jarvis (*Yesterday and Today in Sinai*, 1931, and *Three Deserts*, 1936) knew the deserts of Egypt intimately in the last decades before the motor replaced the camel.

Index

INDEX